My Life Is Full Of Gristle

Gordon Kirkland

Other Books by Gordon Kirkland

- Justice Is Blind – And Her Dog Just Peed In My Cornflakes[1]
- Never Stand Behind A Loaded Horse[2]
- When My Mind Wanders It Brings Back Souvenirs[3]
- I Think I'm Having One Of Those Decades
- I May Be Big But I Didn't Cause That Solar Eclipse
- Holly Jolly Frivolity
- Crossbow
- The Plight Before Christmas

---

[1] Recipient of the 2000 Stephen Leacock Award of Merit for Humour

[2] Recipient of the 2005 Stephen Leacock Award of Merit for Humour

[3] Recipient of the 2006 Stephen Leacock Award of Merit for Humour

My Slice Of Life Is Full Of Gristle

Gordon Kirkland

At Large Publishing

©2012, Gordon Kirkland.

All rights reserved, including the right to reproduce this book or portions thereof in any form whatsoever.

ISBN-13: 978-1469918334
ISBN-10: 1469918331

Front Cover Photo
© Can Stock Photo Inc./mflippo

Readers Comments About Other Books By Gordon Kirkland

A small selection of comments about some of Gordon Kirkland's other books.

When My Mind Wanders It Brings Back Souvenirs

"I couldn't put it down, I kept on repeating to myself: OK, just one more column, just one more... until I finished the whole thing without noticing."

"Charming, witty, the kind of intelligent humor that makes you laugh aloud."

"*I came across your book When My Mind Wanders It Brings Backs Souvenirs, I have not laughed so hard in years! About half way through it, I started to panic that the "party was almost over", so I immediately went in search of more of your work.*

Holly Jolly Frivolity

"Normally, I read holiday books around the holidays, but Gordon's light-hearted look at his Christmases past are good reading any time of year. Not only are his stories funny, I could completely relate to his predicaments, whether it's attempting to get the tree in the stand or learning just how much his kids listen to him when they shouldn't be. I would recommend this book to anyone who likes to laugh."

Crossbow

"If you like a good page turner, with well rendered characters and numerous plot twists - then Crossbow is for you".

"Gordon has crafted a fascinating story with quirky characters everywhere, and he tells the story in the same hilarious way as his humor essays. It should appeal to readers who enjoy having their tales told by a unique voice."

The Plight Before Christmas

"This was just a totally magical holiday read from page one all the way to 'The End'...in fact, I didn't really want it to end!"

"It's one of those books that will forever change the way you think about Christmas...in a very heart-warming but LMAO kinda way."

"If Norman Rockwell had used words instead of pictures to capture times of long ago, he would have been Gordon Kirkland. THE PLIGHT BEFORE CHRISTMAS is a sweet and tender holiday story with some worthy lessons well placed."

To my wife Diane who has stood by me "in thickness and in health" for nearly forty years. She can tenderize the gristle in any slice of life.

Gordon Kirkland is the award-winning and best-selling author of eight other books. He is a three-time recipient of the Stephen Leacock Award of Merit as a finalist for the Leacock Medal for his collections of humorous essays.

He has garnered a very large and loyal fan base in the United States and Canada, as well as elsewhere around the world.

For 13 years he wrote the syndicated newspaper column, *Gordon Kirkland At Large*, which appeared in numerous papers in both Canada and the United States. His first five books of humorous essays were stories that got their start in the newspaper column. A sixth book, *Holly Jolly Frivolity* was produced based on some of his holiday themed columns as well as other material including rewritten holiday songs.

In addition, he has written two novels, *Crossbow* and *The Plight Before Christmas*.

Gordon Kirkland has been a workshop leader and keynote speaker at dozens of writer's conferences, festivals, and university programs over the past fifteen years. This includes three sessions of the University of Dayton's Erma Bombeck Writer's Workshop, six years on the faculty of the Southern California Writer's Conference, as well as many more. He has lectured at Simon Fraser University (Vancouver, BC), Ball State University (Muncie, Indiana), The University of Georgia (Athens, GA), and Florida First Coast Community College (Jacksonville, FL.)

In 2009, Kirkland was one of the stars of The 3-Day Novel, a television series on Canada's BookTelevision, in which 12 Canadian writers were locked in a large bookstore with the task of writing a full novel in just 72 hours. This was carried out under the watchful eye of television cameras, store customers, and with numerous interruptions aimed at breaking the writers' trains of thought. He wrote the first draft of his novel *Crossbow* during the show.

In 2011, the Kindle versions of several of Gordon's books attained best-seller status, with *The Plight Before Christmas* peaking in the top 100 of all books available for the Kindle. *Holly Jolly Frivolity* and *The*

Plight Before Christmas were the two top selling humorous Christmas books for the Kindle.

Gordon lives in Pitt Meadows, BC with, Diane, and their adopted Labrador Retriever, Tara. They have two grown sons.

My Slice Of Life Is Full Of Gristle

Introduction and Acknowledgements	19
Is That A Needle In Your Pocket Or Are You Just Happy To See Me	23
You Could Say I'm Unfeeling	27
Reverse Television Miniaturization	31
She Enjoys The Show Even If The Cast Are All Bird-Brained	35
Snakes Don't Love Me... The Bible Tells Me So	39
Aging Is Easier On The Buddy System	43
I Don't Write Mushy Stuff... Maybe I Should	47
Stonehenge Will Have To Wait A Bit Longer For Me	51
Rebels Without A Clue	57
I'm Going On Vacation. It's Time To Hit Me With A Big Bill	61

I'll Have An Omelet And A Large Order Of Shut-Up For The Waitress	65
Bringing New Meaning To 'Stalking'	69
Driven To Desperation	73
Did I Really Say That?	77
Flight Delays Of Mice And Men	81
Something A Little Nuts For Your Dog	85
Are You Being Serviced?	89
Prison Reform Starts At The Bottom	93
Canada: Where Consenting Numismatics Go To Party	97
Pop Goes The Tenor	101
Does An Author Poop In The Woods? ...Almost	105
Proof That The End Is Near	109
And I Thought I Could Eat	113
It Ain't Me, Babe	117
A Weird World Of Sports	121
Back In (And Out Of) The Saddle Again	125
A Week With Scots and Scotch	129
What Goes Up Must Come Down... Somewhere	133
I Hope My Characters Follow Instructions Better Than I Do	137

Typically Atypical	145
I'm Stuck Thinking About The "C" Word	151
House Parties Are Dangerous When You Are Me	155
WTF Do They Do There For Excitement?	161
This Little Light Of Mine	165
Does Medicare Pay Amateur Physicians?	171
A Family Can Turn You Green	177
It's Just A Dream... I Hope	181
All My Actions Can Have An Unequal And Unpredictable Reaction	185
Hopefully When He Becomes A Doctor He'll Have A Roof Over His Head.	189
I Hate Those Fish-Lip Kisses	193
Thankfully The Sharks Weren't In The Mood For Pâté de Gord Gras	197
Dogs That Have Owned Me	203

Introduction and Acknowledgements

I said I wasn't going to do this. I guess I should have said "probably."

After I stopped writing my syndicated newspaper column in 2007, I thought I was finished with writing short essays. My first six books were all based on the stories I told in the column, and then I turned to writing novels.

Something kept haunting me about the essay form. On a regular basis I would find myself saying, that would have made a great column. My life, at least the slices of it that I have shared with my readers for the past eighteen years, has seemed to have been one humorous short story after another.

I often wonder if these sorts of things happen to other people, or if some great mystical power has centered me out for this ever so special treatment.

In 2011, we took four of my previous books of short humorous essays and made them available for the owners of the Kindle electronic reader. During the newspaper days I was often told that my column was only good for kindling. I expected to sell three or four copies of these books, because they had been available in bookstores for several years, and sales had long ago peaked. Sure enough, in January we sold three copies. But then it started growing. By December thousands of copies were selling every month. People started asking me when I would be writing a new collection.

I thought about replying with the answer to that question that my friend Dave Barry uses when it is posed to him, "Sometime after I am dead." I would have used it, but I have a hard and fast policy to never steal anything from Dave. As he says, we are both maturity impaired, so we have lots of our own material to use without borrowing a cup of silliness from each other.

As you can plainly see, I gave in. I started writing a couple of essays, and before long it felt like I had run into an old friend on the street. While I love writing novels, these short essays are a lot of fun to write. I hope they are as much fun to read.

As always there are people to thank when publishing a book.

My friends in the writing community have been great allies throughout the years, providing encouragement and advice. Ridley Pearson, Dave Barry, Bruce Cameron, Nancy Warren, Barry Eisler, Lynn Johnston, and Tracy Beckerman have always been there for me, and I hope in some small way I am able to return the favors.

My friend Lars always knows when it's time to stop and smell a cup of coffee or two (or if it's after noon, a more potent consumable.)

My older son, Mike has been an incredible help this past year, acting as my assistant, and taking care of all of the conversion to the electronic books. I couldn't have handled the technology side of things without him.

My younger son, Brad has been living in England for the past two years and will be there for another three. He completed his Master's degree (cited "With Distinction" no less), and is now working on his PhD. I am incredibly proud of him and thankful for our long distance calling plan that lets us keep having long conversations about history and literature.

My 'long-suffering' wife Diane has been at my side since our first date on September 11, 1971. She is my world.

And finally thanks to you, my readers, whether you are one of the ones who have been along for this ride since the beginning in 1994, or if you have just joined the party now. There would be no point working on these books, if it weren't for all of you.

Is That A Needle In Your Pocket Or Are You Just Happy To See Me

It's no secret that I enjoy making people laugh. They can laugh with me at some of the strange and unusual events that I write about, and they can laugh at me, when I describe some of the things that go on in my life. OK, so those things also make people sympathize with my wife for having put up with me for over thirty-three years. As Lynn Johnston, the creator of the For Better Or For Worse comic strip says, she likes to read my writing, but she wouldn't want to be married to me.

A lot of women feel that way.

During the years that I wrote a syndicated column I produced over six hundred and fifty 700 to 800-word flights of fancy. When you multiply that by the number of papers it ran in, and that by the circulation of those papers, it means that between 1994 and 2007, millions of women felt sorry for my wife, have been glad they weren't married to me, and were left feeling a little bit better about their own marital choices. No doubt, just as many men have felt better about themselves, because they know that I can be counted on to do something to make their wives feel thankful about marrying them, and not someone like me.

It's a public service I'm happy to provide. You're welcome.

I learned a lot over the years. For example:

- If I say that having a colonoscopy didn't hurt until they shoved a tripod through that particular opening to steady the camera, there are some people who will actually believe that a tripod is used during the procedure.

- It's OK to make fun of some professions, but there are those who will run crying to the advertising departments of the papers if I focus on their line of work.

- You get fewer threatening letters joking about motorcycle gangs or the mob than the Red Hat Society.

- Political humor is best left to the experts – the politicians.
- Using Webster's spelling, which results in dropping the 'u' in 'colour' or 'flavour' will cause at least one retired Canadian English teacher to write a letter of complaint every month or so.

For the most part, I have enjoyed my interactions with my readers. There have been a few occasions that have been a bit on the weird side, though. A couple of those were examples why, in the minds of writers, the scariest book Stephen King ever wrote was, *Misery*. It only took one, slightly wacko fan to show me the wisdom of an unlisted telephone number.

Thankfully, laughter is something most people want in their lives, even someone like Patrick Knight, spent his final days living in Huntsville, Texas.

According to a Reuters' news item Mr. Knight solicited jokes on the Internet, in order to come up with the best one to tell just before receiving a lethal injection in the Texas execution room.

"I'll be enjoying my last days on Earth," Knight wrote on a Web site that was established by a friend in order to collect material for what will have to be the shortest comedy career on record.

Somehow, I don't think the two people Knight murdered in 1991 had the opportunity for one last bit of witticism before he shot them and left their bodies in a ditch near Amarillo.

Texas Department of Criminal Justice spokeswoman Michelle Lyons said, that he wanted to keep his execution light, adding, "We've certainly had some people who have recited a poem or a Bible verse, some people who have asked forgiveness or who pray. This is, to my knowledge, the first time anybody has told a joke as their last words."

Ms. Lyons also said that Knight was given the opportunity to tell his last joke, but that the prison staff was not allowed to participate. As she put it, "Knock-knock jokes are out."

I suppose I could have been charitable and sent something along to ease them man's final moments. I heard one last week that would absolutely slay him.

Oops. Look at the calendar. Too late.

You Could Say I'm Unfeeling

Having a spinal cord injury definitely has its downside. In fact, I often fall on my downside, which is why I have Tara, my Labrador retriever assistance dog. She can help me back to my feet if and when my downside hit's the ground's upside.

It's now been twenty-one years since I was involved in what I like to call my golfing accident. I was on my way to play golf when another driver thought it was more important to find the cassette tape he had dropped on the floor of his car, than to watch where he was going.

Unfortunately, I had stopped between him and where he was going.

I've often been told how lucky I am. I still have enough feeling below the waist to allow me to walk with crutches clipped to my arms. I have enough use of my right leg to drive a car, although because of the great loss of function on my left side, I am prohibited from driving a car with a standard transmission.

I think that's why my wife would like to buy a sports car with a standard transmission. She knows that I couldn't drive it, and all the fun would be hers.

There is one rather large upside to losing much of the surface sensation on my legs. From time to time I will see a large bruise on my leg and think, "Gee, I bet that really hurts."

I learned a few weeks ago that not feeling an injury to my legs may not be the big advantage that I thought it was.

It started out fairly innocuously. I didn't change the position of my legs enough during a four-hour drive.

Anyone else would feel their legs starting to get uncomfortable after that length of time, and I am usually pretty good about remembering to move from time to time. For some reason on this occasion, I forgot.

As I drove, my leg rubbed on a rough patch on the inside of my boot. Two blisters developed on my calf. I didn't know they were there, until I noticed them later that night, once again thinking, "Gee, I bet those hurt."

I didn't think of them again until four days later. As I was getting ready for bed at about one o'clock in the morning, I noticed that my leg was bright red from the knee to the ankle. Clearly, I had developed a rather severe infection, thanks to the blisters, but still did not feel it. One look told me that it was a fairly serious infection, so I decided to drive myself to the emergency ward to have it checked out.

I spent the next several days visiting the hospital twice a day for an intravenous injection of antibiotics. I had to walk around with the IV connection taped to my wrist. At a party an American friend of mine asked what it was.

"Well," I whispered to him, "because I've eaten a lot of pancakes over the years, and there is currently a maple syrup shortage in my country, I'm part of a top-secret Canadian syrup reclamation program. They've tapped me like a maple tree."

For a moment I thought he was going to buy it, but then he remembered who he was talking to. It's hard to pull the wool over someone's eyes, no matter how gullible they might be, when you have a reputation for being a professional smart-ass.

It probably serves me right that the next day I noticed a rash developing in places that I can feel. (Yes, there too.) My body decided that it didn't really like all of those antibiotics that were being pumped into me. It retaliated by making me allergic to them. I am already allergic to two other types of antibiotics. I'm starting to run out of options.

In order to combat the allergic reaction the doctor put me on steroids and antihistamines, both of which would make me fail a urine test at the Olympics. I guess it will give me another reason that I'll have to rule out competing in the Winter Games.

And now I'll never get elected to the Baseball Hall of Fame.

Reverse Television Miniaturization

When Diane and I were first married the average church mouse was significantly more affluent than we were.

We were lucky. We managed to get an apartment on the campus of the university we were attending that was fully furnished, and its proximity to our classes eliminated the need for a car. 'Fully furnished' meant that it came with a bed, and the standard living room furnishings. It did not include one truly important piece of furniture.

A television.

We got someone's cast-off set that was made roughly the same year as Diane and I were made. It was a black and white model and housed in a large wooden console. It took five minutes for the tubes to warm up enough to create a picture. Luckily we lived on the fourteenth floor of the building. By running a wire to one of the curtain rods, we were able to almost make out the picture on two or three channels.

After a few months, we decided that we were either going to have to spend a little of the money we had gotten as wedding gifts on a TV, or go blind trying to watch the set we had. We returned all our bottles, dug around in the sofa for loose change, withdrew a little cash from the bank, and bought a twelve-inch black and white TV. Of course, in that small apartment, a twelve-inch TV looked much bigger.

Watching a hockey game was an effort. You just had to guess where the puck was and which one of the miniscule players was going to take a shot.

That set did us for three years. By then our financial situation had improved significantly. We had bought our first house, and we were now better off than two out of three church mice.

I tried to watch one of the inaugural Canada Cup hockey games on that set. Canada in white jerseys played Sweden in Yellow jerseys. On a black and white set, especially one that small, it was impossible to tell the teams apart. The time had come for a color TV, but our bank account had other ideas.

Not even our bottle return fund or the sofa cushions could make up the required financial resources for a color TV. As we sat squinting at the small set one night, an ad solved the problem. We discovered furniture rentals.

For a few dollars a month, we had color TV in time to watch the final game of the Canada Cup series. The tiny black and white was relegated to the bedroom. We really didn't care how pasty the late-night news anchor looked staring out at us through the snowy static.

Over the years we've owned several televisions, each larger than its predecessor. Our last TV was a thirty-two-inch Sony Trinitron that we bought in 1994. After trying to lift it onto its stand, I determined that Sony had misspelled the name of the set. It should have been Trinaton, because the thing felt light it weighed at least a ton.

In the small living rooms we've had since then, that TV seemed massive. When we moved a few years ago, we discovered that putting it into a seventeen-foot by twenty-eight-foot room made it look like the old twelve inch black and white we had started with over thirty years ago.

Thankfully, we no longer have to search under the sofa cushions for change, to help pay for a new set. Still, we didn't want to pay more than we had to for the one we picked out. As a result we did something we swore we would never do.

Along enough other bargain hunters to populate a small city, we went to an electronics superstore on Boxing Day. Some people had been camped outside the store since the middle of the afternoon on Christmas Day.

We now have a fifty-inch TV gracing the corner of the room. I no longer have to worry about trying to determine which team is which in a hockey game. I could probably do without being able to count the goalie's nose hairs, though.

I thought that set would prove to be adequate for several years to come. Unfortunately, my buddy Lars went out and upped the ante by buying a sixty-inch set. Now I feel so inferior when I watch a game on his set, and then return to watch something on our miniscule fifty-inch.

When I mentioned my inferiority complex to Diane she gave me one of those wifely looks that immediately let me know where she thought a larger TV might be on the list of upcoming household acquisitions.

…and she did it in high-definition.

She Enjoys The Show Even If The Cast Are All Bird-Brained

Looking back over the thirteen years I wrote the syndicated newspaper column, I can see that my dogs follow only marriage and parenthood in subject frequency.

For the first many years, I wrote about Nipper, also known as 'the dumbest dog to ever get lost on a single flight of stairs.' She was loving, loyal, and slightly less intelligent than a sack full of rusty hammers.

Tara, my current canine roommate, is at the other end of the dog intellectual spectrum, but can be just as entertaining. She may be able to navigate a flight of stairs on her own, but she comes with her own set of quirky behaviors.

One of the great things about owning a dog is seeing just how easy they are to entertain. Children need hundreds of dollars' worth of video games, a wide-screen plasma television, and an unlimited supply of food. Tara, on the other paw, can be entertained for hours with nothing more than a biscuit hidden inside a rubber chew toy.

The most elaborate electronic toy I've bought for my dog is a laser pointer. Initially, it was used to train her to pick up objects and bring them to me. I soon discovered that she got a lot more enjoyment out of chasing the little red dot up and down the hall. I can waste a good half hour directing her throughout the house with it.

It took a while, but she's finally learned that no matter how hard she runs at that little dot, she won't catch it by slamming her nose into the wall where it's shining. Now she'll charge down the hall after the light, and stop just inches from the wall.

The game of attack the vacuum cleaner usually only lasts until her tongue makes contact with the rotary brush head.

I'm used to having her asleep under my feet at my desk most of the day, but for the past few days, she has been heading out to the living room while I worked. I have two books coming out this year, so my concentration has been on my computer not on whatever was holding the dog's attention.

My curiosity finally got the better of me, when she didn't come running when I rattled her dog biscuit box. I found her sitting at the front window, looking as mesmerized as a moviegoer staring at an IMAX screen. She didn't even turn to see me when I came into the room.

Apparently, I've been replaced by the cast of her own private theatrical production.

About thirty feet from the window is a large flowering cherry tree. A few days ago I hung two bird feeders from the branches of the tree. It took a day or two before the birds discovered them, but now the tree is filled with chickadees, juncos, wrens, finches and sparrows. Two black squirrels and a very obese gray squirrel have also discovered the feeders.

Tara thinks they have all come to entertain her.

Occasionally, I will hear her get upset and start barking. I've learned that usually means that the neighbor's cat has decided to venture into our yard in hopes of picking up a bucket of popcorn chickadee, or even a family pack of squirrel delight.

Tara's reaction sounds like an irate theater patron who has just had someone stand up between her and the stage.

"Down in front! Down in front!"

I discovered that she doesn't like her version of horror movies, though.

She was in the car with me last weekend when I went to one of those high-pressure car washes. Having the whole car go dark and claustrophobic when the soapsuds covered the windows was frightening enough for her, but when jets of water started shooting at the car from all sides, I thought the dog was going to have a coronary. I'm glad that Labrador retrievers are very particular about where they take care of their bodily functions.

I don't know how she'd react to an upholstery shampooer.

Snakes Don't Love Me...
The Bible Tells Me So

OK, I am on record as being willing to admit that snakes are something that I just don't like. I'm also secure enough in my manhood to admit that if one sneaks up on me, I can scream like a little girl until it is either deaf or out of sight.

This morning, when I checked Reuters' news stories from the past week, I got more snake news than I could ever need or want.

When I was three or four years old, my dog cornered a snake under our summer cottage. It was about to bite, so I did what any dog-loving kid would do in that situation. I tried to grab it. When you are three or four years old, you are not necessarily the best candidate to go around grabbing snakes. Snakes are much better at grabbing three or four year olds.

Because rattlesnakes had been reported in the area, I was rushed off to the hospital. Well, perhaps 'rushed' is too strong a word. We were a mile by boat from town and our old cedar strip runabout only had a seven horsepower outboard, so I guess you could say I was moseyed off to the hospital.

It wasn't a rattlesnake that bit me. Still, it did a pretty good number on my fingers, two of which fit conveniently into its mouth.

My mother was embarrassed to have to admit that she had raised a son who would put his fingers in the way of a snake's mouth. She was even more embarrassed when, thanks to a neighbor, the next week's local paper ran a headline that read "Gull Lake Boy Bitten By Snake."

I guess it was a slow news week.

It was that event that put the severe dislike for snakes into my psyche. Nearly half a century later, I still don't like to think about snakes and, after reading Reuters this morning, I find myself checking under my desk every few minutes to make sure that there are no snakes in the vicinity.

That cable between my computer and the monitor certainly gave me quite a start.

When I was in Southeast Asia in 1990 I was taken on a sightseeing trip by boat up the Chao Phraya River. No one told me that at the end of the trip we'd be stopping for lunch at a snake farm, or that there was a chance I would be lunch.

Four men carried out a massive python and put it down on the ground not far enough from my seat. It headed straight in my direction. I realized then that sitting in a corner had not been the best option for a speedy escape, should one be needed.

At that moment, one was very much needed.

It seemed like they stopped the snake just microns before it reached me. In reality it was probably still about six feet away, but another inch or two and I would have left visible evidence of my visit that someone would have to clean up.

In the news stories, a spa in Israel is offering massages by snakes. The spa owner, who charges the equivalent of seventy dollars for this horror, points out that they are nonpoisonous king and corn snakes. The one that bit me so many years ago wasn't poisonous either. My first thought was, with the dress code for a massage being what it is, who knows what a king snake might grab.

She says they very soothing and good for aching muscles and joints. I know for a fact that it would certainly loosen up my sphincter muscles.

Reuters also reported that Malaysia's "Snake King," who spent twenty-five years mesmerizing scorpions and snakes during live performances died last month after being bitten by a king cobra. He probably had just enough time to question the rationale behind his career choice.

Perhaps the most horrific snake story of them all was about the 23-foot python that ate eleven guard dogs trying to protect an orchard in Malaysia. I guess there weren't any three or four year olds around to protect the dogs.

Or maybe there once were...

Aging Is Easier On The Buddy System

There is definitely something to be said for getting together with old friends. I have a few and don't get to see them often enough. I had the chance to sit with one of them the other night for the first time in a couple of years. The thing about old friends is you really don't have to see each other every day. A year, two, or five can go by and, when you do share an evening together, it as though you saw each other a day or two ago.

Paul Simon wrote, "Can you imagine us years from today, sharing a park bench quietly. How terribly strange to be seventy. Old friends, memory brushes the same years, silently sharing the same fears."

Dave Barry points out that he and I are both suffering from 'maturity impairment.' It's one of the prerequisites for doing this job. It's probably a prerequisite for people who remain my friends for over thirty years. It's certainly the case with my long-time friend, Roy. Probably one of the few things my wife and his ex-wife would agree on is that the two of us share an equally defective maturity gene.

Roy and I have a decade and a bit before we will be seventy and sitting on a park bench, but whether you are fifty-eight, seventy-three, or a hundred and three, old friends are something that makes life just a little more bearable, and a whole lot more enjoyable.

Thirty three years ago, Roy and I were young men, just starting out in life. We were both students at York University in Toronto. Now we are old friends, and our memories have been brushed by the same years.

I've written about Roy before. He's the one who challenged me to a duel, or to be more accurate double dog dared me to a duel in 1974. It would have been rude not to accept, so I found myself facing him on a dusty street in Scarborough, Ontario, armed with well-shaken bottles of champagne.

We each ended up with a puddle of champagne at our feet. I've always maintained that Roy's puddle contained more than champagne, because my cork came closer to connecting with his head. He disputes it and now neither of us knows where to find the key witnesses who might have been sober enough to tell fact from fiction, and champagne from champagne mixed with second hand beer.

Once you are drunk enough to conclude that a champagne duel in the middle of suburbia might be a good idea, you really should stop drinking.

These days we live over two thousand miles apart. We can't get together for a spontaneous champagne duel whenever the whim might arise. Thankfully, the cost of long distance telephone calls has dropped to the point where we can talk about doing it.

The other thing about old friends is they are the ones who you can turn to, no matter what is going on in your life. After over thirty years, we have experienced the good and the bad in each other's lives. We know when to laugh at something, and more importantly, we know when the other guy really needs to laugh.

A couple of years ago, Roy went through a divorce. People talk about how a divorce can be messy, frustrating, and emotionally devastating. The bombing of Hiroshima was probably messy, frustrating, and emotionally devastating. Roy's divorce was on an entirely different scale.

Roy got through it with his lawyer, who he paid big bucks to advise him that he was going to be skewered by the process, his accountant, who he paid big bucks to advise him that he was going to be financially skewered, and me. Every male going through a divorce should have an old friend who knows what buttons to push to make him laugh at the situation.

It's the least I could do.

Down the road we'll probably be like the two old friends Simon and Garfunkel sang about, 'sharing a park bench quietly.' I wonder if we'll still be strong enough to push the cork out of a champagne bottle, should we decide to have another duel.

I Don't Write Mushy Stuff... Maybe I Should

I spent six years on the faculty of a writer's conference in southern California. The conference ran every President's Day weekend in San Diego. As a Canadian, I think it is my prerogative that, if I have to be someplace in February, it had better be warm.

Churchill, Manitoba is definitely not on my list.

I would spend the weekend with a couple of hundred writers. Some are published and successful, some are hoping to be published and will someday be successful, and some can barely put two words together, but will probably end up more successful than all of us put together.

One year, I hoped that one of my best friends in this business could have joined me in San Diego, but there was something she seemed to think was more important to do. Normally, I could count on Nancy Warren to gladly spend a weekend hanging out, drinking copious amounts of recreational fluids, and laughing ourselves silly.

What could be more important than that?

Nancy and I just bring out the best in one another. The trouble is our best looks a lot like the next guy's certifiable insanity.

There's one writer's conference that will probably never invite us back, but that's a whole other story, and I have promised Nancy to never discuss it in a non-fiction book.

My weekend was a lot of fun, filled with good conversation, sleep deprivation, and yes, a fair amount of recreational liquid. Nancy's weekend landed her on the front of the New York Times. Thankfully, it was for her writing, not for some cross-country crime spree.

I don't write the sort of books that will be texts in some future university course about the great classics of the Twenty-First Century. Nancy writes romance novels. Bodices burst and bosoms heave. Some are tame; some are what are called 'erotic women's fiction.' I doubt if she thinks they'll be on the syllabus, either.

I know that I will never be a character in anything Nancy writes, even though under all this flab, I look just like one of those romance novel cover models.

The description of her book, Indulge, says, "Fabulous in bed...summed up John Dennis's thoughts about his fling with Hurricane Mercedes. Which was the problem. Too often they indulged in dessert...instead of dinner."

I get all tingly just thinking about it.

The most erotic thing I ever wrote was about watching a German Shepherd jump from the back of a pickup truck to join a Labrador Retriever in the back of another truck for a bit of canine "dessert."

Despite writing in very different genres, the unwavering view of our books was best summed up by one of my sons. When he saw Nancy's book on the table in our living room he said, "Just looking at it makes me feel dirty." When he sees one of my books, he says, "Just looking at it makes me feel the need for therapy."

It was one of her books and how she spent the weekend that put her on the front of the New York Times. She blew off a weekend in San Diego with me, to launch a new book, *Speed Dating*, in Daytona during NASCAR's biggest race.

Romance novels meet NASCAR for a meaningful relationship.

She launched the book amid an actual speed dating event in Daytona. For the uninitiated, speed dating is when people sit down across the table from a prospective love interest. After five minutes they move on to the next miniature meaningful relationship. In a NASCAR speed dating event they do it all in team jackets, ball caps, and beer bellies.

I've never been a huge car racing fan. A NASCAR race looks more like a whole bunch of drivers lined up under the motto, 'Step on the gas and keep turning left."

It reminds me of my wife before I got GPS installed the car.

In a business that is driven by publicity I'm a little envious of Nancy today. On the other hand, I guess I should be thankful too. In a Six Degrees of Kevin Bacon sort of way, I'm now just one step from the front page of the New York Times.

And NASCAR too. Whoo-eee!

Stonehenge Will Have To Wait A Bit Longer For Me

I have always wanted to visit Stonehenge. This desire isn't so much for the opportunity to dance naked in the circle and get in touch with the Celtic side of my heritage. It's more just to see it because it is there, it's been there for a long time, and no one really knows how it got there.

Of course I could also say the same about some of the stains in the living room carpet.

My Slice Of Life Is Full Of Gristle

My opportunity came a couple of years ago. Diane and I headed off to see Jolly Old England, in part to spend some time with our son who is living there, and partially to see some of the countryside. During our stay we visited ruins of ancient abbeys, a few castles, and prepared for a day that would include a visit to Windsor Castle, Bath, and Stonehenge.

We made arrangements with the tour company to give me the front seat on the bus. Between my crutches and my leg brace, it is somewhat difficult for me to get into bus seats further down the aisle. An American woman, who clearly wanted to perpetuate the stereotype that American tourists have overseas, complained bitterly that she did not get the seat I was occupying. She spent the first leg of the trip scowling at me.

We traveled through the countryside with a very genial tour guide regaling is with stories about the history of the area, and the late Queen Mother's penchant for a nip of gin or twelve.

When we arrived at Windsor, we walked through the ancient town, and onto the grounds of the castle, still in use by the Royals as a weekend getaway. Apparently during the plagues of the late 16th Century, Queen Elizabeth I, stayed at Windsor to escape the disease. Anyone who arrived at the gates from London were to be hanged immediately to prevent the possible transmission of the disease to Her Majesty.

I think the American woman from the bus would have nominated me for that fate.

I decided not to venture inside the castle because of all of the stairs. Diane went in while I explored the grounds. We arranged to meet back at the bus at the appointed time.

I got to the bus before Diane and waited... and waited. I was a bit worried because Diane can get lost walking in a straight line. Somehow she was not born with the ability to navigate without several maps and a GPS.

The other passengers had all arrived, and the American woman was eyeing my seat.

After a few more minutes, a policewoman walked up to me and asked, "Are you Gordon Kirkland?"

I figured that being a visitor in a foreign country, I probably should come clean and admit to it. She then told me that there had been an accident, and that Diane had been injured.

Naturally, I asked the policewoman to take me to Diane, and was told, "No. We have to wait forty-five minutes, because the changing of the guard ceremony has started and we can't get through the gates."

The police woman couldn't tell me if Diane was even conscious, but she did know that paramedics were with her, and that she had somehow fallen down a flight of stone stairs. Let's face it, when a 50-something woman goes up against a 400-something set of stairs, the stairs are going to win.

I spoke with the tour guide, and it was determined that the best thing for all concerned would be if they left for the rest of their tour. Overhearing us, the American woman immediately said, "Oh good. Now I can have the front seat."

I normally just use a look to convey my feelings in that sort of a situation, but I looked at her and said, "I'm so glad that my wife being injured has made things better for you."

Her husband and children had all walked away from her. He came over and apologized for what his wife had said. I told him to tell her that when she gets into that seat to bend over as far as she could and shove her head the rest of the way through her rectum.

A police car eventually came and got me and drove me onto the grounds of Windsor Castle to the spot where Diane was. The paramedics had gotten her into an ambulance and were making her breath nitrous oxide – laughing gas. We were taken to a hospital, where it was determined that Diane had broken one arm in two places, chipped a bone in her knee, and broken a couple of fingers on the other hand. Halfway there the nitrous oxide kicked in and I was faced with my wife alternating between crying and giggling.

I hadn't seen yo-yo emotions like that since her heady days of menopause.

Needless to say, I still haven't made it to see Stonehenge, and I'm still not certain that Diane didn't throw herself off down the stairs just to prevent me from deciding to dance naked in the circle.

Rebels Without A Clue

Over the years, I have had several interactions with gang members of various types. Many years ago, we were invited to the wedding of one of my wife's coworkers. She was marrying into a family. While everyone who gets married enters a family, in this case the family was more like the one led Don Corleone in *The Godfather*.

We got the sense the invitation was an offer we couldn't refuse. I spent the entire reception waiting to see if someone would get wacked.

I've also known a lot of bikers over the years. We have a large chapter of the Hell's Angels not too far from here, and I often see them around town. I've talked to quite a few at self-serve gas stations, or in line-ups at the grocery store. For the most part they are pleasant enough, although I wouldn't want to think about what would happen if I knocked over one of their bikes in the parking lot. I also make sure my hand is nowhere near the horn when I am behind one at a traffic light.

Gang activity is not just an inner city nuisance. Suburbia is far from immune. I recently witnessed the scourge of gang behavior in my little town.

I attended a community fundraising event. They invited me to sign books during the evening and I donated a sizable portion of my royalties to their cause. Other area artists were there doing the same thing. All would have gone smoothly, except one of our most visible local gangs decided to crash the event.

They strode in with that peculiar gait that gang members often use these days. For many in the inner city gangs, that stride becomes part of their persona thanks to a bullet entering some part of their lower extremities. Apparently, it's a badge of honor. Even with my crutches, I think I could probably take them in a footrace.

The event was supposed to start at 5:30 PM, but several gang members arrived at 5:00 and demanded to be let in so they could scope out the best table, save seats for their compadres, and let everyone know that the rules for the evening did not apply to them. They even demanded that the bartender, who was trying to get his beer cooler organized, stop what he was doing and serve them.

Beside me, at the table where I was signing books, a young Chinese girl was doing oriental calligraphy. She wrote people's names in Chinese characters, using ancient looking brushes and ink she mixed on the spot. I'm not convinced that what she wrote for me was actually my name. There seems to be a lot more detail than might be expected for just my first name. My bet is that says something along the lines of 'big fat white guy.'

She had a cup in front of her for donations. Over the evening, the cup filled quite nicely. Several of the gang members had her write their names, but not one dime went into the cup from their pockets.

A local potter was selling beautifully crafted bowls and other items. Each piece was unique, and clearly took a great deal of time and care to craft. A gang member knocked one of his pieces to the floor, shattering it. There wasn't even a word of apology, as the offender walked away.

I guess when you're surrounded by your homies, an apology might seem like a sign of weakness.

I understand this gang has opened chapters all over North America and beyond. After my experience encountering them on the weekend, I would recommend that you be very wary if you ever run into a pack of them on the loose.

They're easy enough to spot. That gait they use probably has more to do with bunions than bullets. Most are women who qualified for membership in AARP when the first Bush was still vice-president. Their drug of choice is more likely to be Metamucil® than cocaine. Their gang colors are bright purple, with outrageous red hats. The local leader's hat was so ridiculously massive that it looked like something from a Camilla Parker-Bowles garage sale.

Granny rebels without a cause.

I'm Going On Vacation. It's Time To Hit Me With A Big Bill

I'm leaving on vacation tomorrow, so we all know what that means.

Something went horribly wrong yesterday.

The furnace died. It made an odd buzzing sound every couple of seconds, but it would not produce anything resembling warmth. A friend of mine says the same thing about his ex-wife.

The pilot light was lit, which was a relief. It's not that I am afraid to light it. It's just that it sends my wife into full blown panic mode whenever she has to think about fire and gas at the same time. She experienced a rather dramatic multiple house-leveling gas explosion just before we were married. If the only thing standing between her and starvation was the need to light a gas barbecue, she would go on a hunger strike.

I knew that this was a job that was going to require that I mobilize my full array of handyman skills.

I flicked the switch off and on a couple of times. Then I banged on the side of it twice. I even tried reasoning with it saying, "Come on. You can't do this today. I've got hotel bills and car rental fees to pay this week."

You just can't reason with a furnace that's gone cold. (My friend says that about his ex-wife, too.)

When none of those things worked, I knew it was time to bring out the power tools, so I picked up my trusty six-inch reciprocating telephone receiver and called someone who actually possessed some potentially useful furnace repair skills.

While we waited for him to arrive, Diane and I wondered whether it was going to be an inexpensive quick fix, or if the furnace had gone where faulty furnaces go when they die. If it was the latter, we decided that we'd use the fireplace to heat the house for the remainder of the year.

When you see a repairman pull into your driveway in a Lincoln Navigator, you can quickly determine that the word inexpensive will not be part of your discussion, no matter how quick a fix is required.

After a few minutes the repairman came into the living room, where I was curled up in the fetal position anticipating the size of the bill. He had a small plastic box in his hand.

"It's the most expensive piece in the unit that's shot," he said.

Now, how did I know he was going to say that? It had nothing to do with ESP. I just knew that, even if he had come into the room carrying a small rubber washer, he'd say, "It's the most expensive piece in the unit that's shot."

Repairmen seem to have a mantra. "It's the computer."

When my car died a couple years ago, I was told, "It's the computer." When my dishwasher stopped, I heard, "It's the computer." I'm surprised that a doctor hasn't held a stethoscope up to my chest and said, "It's the computer."

On the other hand, when my computer died the repairman said something along the lines of, "It's the central core doofangle processing thingy on the heat dissipating mother whatsit."

Actually, he didn't use words like doofangle or thingy. I just zoned out during his explanation because I had no idea what he was talking about, and I knew what was coming next.

"It's the most expensive piece in the unit that's shot."

I'm not even sure if I believe that my furnace has a computer. I think the manufacturers attach a small plastic box that the repairmen can pull off and show to the customers when they say, "It's the most expensive piece in the unit that's shot."

In my case the replacement plastic box cost over $400.00. Even with my math skills, I was able to figure that he'd only need to replace a couple of those a month to pay the lease on the Navigator.

It wasn't enough to spoil the vacation. I'll still be heading out tomorrow. I can still pay for a rental car, but you can be sure it won't be a Lincoln Navigator.

After all, I'm just not in the same income bracket as a furnace repairman.

I'll Have An Omelet And A Large Order Of Shut-Up For The Waitress

I'm sure by now most of you are aware that it takes a lot for me to stop eating before my plate is clear. You just don't become as big for your age as I am by leaving food behind. It probably goes back to my mother admonishing me about starving children in Africa if I didn't clean my plate.

Traveling around the country as much as I do, you get to experience a wide spectrum of service in the hospitality industry. Some of it isn't all that hospitable.

My wife and I recently returned from a week on the road through Arizona and southern Colorado. It was a spectacular trip, and one we had been planning for quite a while. As is the norm with our traveling, we put a couple thousand miles on our rental car in the six days we had it.

We had fantastic food, unusual food, and in one case a burger that tasted like biting into a salt shaker. We also had one meal that, through no fault of the cook, I could not bring myself to finish.

On the plus side, was our first night in Phoenix, when we visited a restaurant that our airline recommended. I'm never overly sure about those recommendations, because the cynic in me thinks that it is just another form of paid advertising. Thankfully, in this case, I was wrong. The food was good, and the service was even better.

Our waiter, who appeared to be about twenty years old, went to great lengths to describe the different items on the menu, which is handy, because I refer to my wife as "the menu re-arranger."

"I'll have the steak special, but instead of the steamed vegetables, can I get a salad? Oh, but I'd like you to leave out the onions, olives, and croutons, and put the dressing on the side. Does that come with cheese in it? If it does, could you put the cheese off to the side, too? Can I get a baked potato instead of the garlic mashed? I don't want any sour cream or other ingredients. Just some butter on the side."

I've seen waiters need three separate sheets of paper, just to take her order.

As we ate our dinner, it became clear that the people at the next table were also menu re-arrangers, and their order had not come as they wished. Their waiter, another young man about the same age as ours, did not get frazzled by the temper tantrum his customers were having about their order. He said that he accepted full responsibility, had his manager come to see them, and wrote off their bill.

I think that might have been the whole point of the tirade.

Obviously, neither of those two young men had been in the business very long, but both were clearly the sort of employee I would want, if I ever completely lost my mind and opened a restaurant.

At the other end of our trip, as we returned home from the airport, we stopped for lunch at a restaurant we have frequented a number of times. We won't eat there again. I'm not even sure if I want to eat again.

Our waiter, served us promptly, and did a good job. It was one of the other staff, who put us off our meals.

As we ate, a waitress, clearly at the other end of the age and professionalism spectrum from the two young men in Phoenix, stood talking loudly to her customers a couple of tables away from ours.

She described burning herself, what it did to the skin on her arm, the infection that ensued, and the need to have one of her fingernails removed. Our whole end of the restaurant was subjected to the minutest details of the after-effect of the burn.

She then moved on to describe someone's surgery to remove a cancerous lump from his back, and detailed how the wound was not healing, leaving a gaping open sore.

I think even my mother would have given me a pass for not cleaning my plate after listening to that, no matter how many starving children there are in Africa.

Bringing New Meaning To 'Stalking'

I went to a hockey game and a lingerie party broke out.

Hockey is not a sport that one might associate with lacy undergarments. In a related point, former Vancouver Canucks player Jeff Cowan was not someone who you'd call a scoring machine. Odd as it may seem, the two came together at a game a couple of years ago.

Cowan was picked up by the Canucks to be a utility player. That's a polite way of saying, he's the guy who will go out and beat the daylights out of an opponent. He hadn't scored a goal since he joined the team. Suddenly, over a period of four games, he scored six times.

The lingerie party broke out after his second goal in a game.

It's a tradition in hockey that if a player scores three goals in a game, referred to as a hat-trick, fans will throw their hats onto the ice. It's highly unlikely that Cowan will ever see the shower of caps, but after that second goal, a fan threw her leopard-print bra onto the ice.

Perhaps she wanted to give him a little uplifting support, or separate him from some of the other boobs in the game.

The Vancouver Canucks may be hoping to hoist the cup, but I think they probably want the Stanley Cup, not a leopard-print C-cup. The referee didn't seem too sure what he should do with it.

We've all been there, haven't we guys?

Many years ago, I went to a playoff hockey game at the old Detroit Olympia. During playoff time, the Red Wings fans have the habit of tossing an octopus onto the ice. I spent the game hoping that, if someone behind me planned to throw an octopus, he would have a decent throwing arm.

In other words, I didn't want to be sitting in front of anyone from the Detroit Tigers.

It's not just a North American phenomenon. Fans of the Chelsea Football Club in England have gotten themselves in a bit of trouble lately over their object throwing antics. Soccer hooliganism runs rampant over there in jolly old England.

I have to be careful to say 'England' and not refer to it as 'Britain.' Last time I mentioned British soccer fans, I received a deluge of mail from Scottish soccer fans, who did not like being lumped in with the English fans. According to them, Scottish soccer fans are gentile and polite.

The Football Association has stated that the throwing of anything at a football match, including celery, is a criminal offence for which you can be arrested and end up with a criminal record.

Yes, I said, "including celery." Apparently, Chelsea's fans have been throwing celery during games for the past twenty years.

Does the brutality of English soccer fans know no bounds? I can understand why the refined Scottish fans wouldn't want to be associated with anything as uncivilized as celery chucking.

The offending vegetable is tossed after the singing of a particularly odd little ditty:

Celery, Celery
If she don't come
I'll tickle her bum
With a lump of celery.

Say what?

This just raises a whole bunch of questions, not the least of which is what does it have to do with soccer?

Is 'a lump of celery' the whole plant, or just one stalk? Are the leaves attached, or has someone taken a knife to it, so it's just the bare stock at the tip? Does the size of your celery really matter? Is this so-called coming and bum-tickling an activity soccer fans in England regularly do in the stands?

If so, where can I get tickets?

Driven To Desperation

Someone asked me the other day if I missed the days when my sons were younger. I have to admit that there are times that I feel a slight twinge of nostalgia, particularly when I see kids heading out to play hockey. Some of my fondest memories are of my days, freezing my butt off in arenas, watching the boys play.

Of course, having a son who played the game twelve months of the year, made it a pretty big part of my life for several years. My olfactory capabilities are still severely impaired because I inhaled too much sweaty locker room air during that period.

My Slice Of Life Is Full Of Gristle

The Surgeon General should put a warning on locker room doors.

A friend of mine sent me an email last week reminding me of a time in my sons' lives I would just as soon forget. He is going through it with his teenage son right now. Just thinking about it can cause one of those full-body shudders.

He was desperate for some help; so desperate in fact, he asked if he could borrow my wife. He's a good friend and all, but even I have my limits. I would never consider lending out my wife, no matter how good a friend he is, or how desperate he might be. He even offered to fly Diane to Toronto, provide her with a chauffeur driven limo, and cover any other expenses she might incur, if she would just do for his son what she did for mine.

He wants her to teach him to drive.

Any parent, who is going through the driver education process with one of their dear young offspring, can sympathize with his situation. I had tried to put it all out my mind, and I wasn't even the one who went out on the practice drives with our boys. My friend is a single parent, so he doesn't have the luxury of a team approach to driver's education. Even though I didn't venture anywhere near the car when it came time to teach our sons, I still had a very important role to serve.

I hosed down the driveway so that the ground would be clean for Diane to kiss when she got out of the car at the end of a session.

My friend learned just how important a service that is when he took his son out for his first drive on Saint Patrick's Day. Old Patrick may have driven the snakes out of Ireland, just so he wouldn't have to teach them how to brake, steer, or change gears.

He said, "When I got home, I almost poisoned myself from all the crud on my driveway as I kissed the ground. I spent the rest of the day trying to disinfect my lips by passing green beer over them, but with only 5% alcohol it takes quite a few pints until you are confident you have killed all the germs.

He may not have needed quite so many pints, but once you get started on the green beer on St. Patrick's Day, you don't need much of an excuse to keep drinking. Actually, he and I have never needed much of an excuse at any time of the year, but that's another story.

My father avoided the whole driver's education debacle with me. He simply refused to have anything to do with it. My mother didn't drive, so she wasn't any help either. I didn't learn to drive until I was twenty-one years old. Since I was already married by then, you can guess who got to teach me to drive, too.

To this day, no one can hit an imaginary brake pedal faster than my wife.

I'm sure that someday my friend will look back on these years with his son and feel the occasional pang of nostalgia. He'll miss some of the more enjoyable activities they do together. Of course, if his mind ever wanders back to the driver's education experience, you can be sure he will have one of those full-body shudders.

He'll also go looking for a green beer or twelve to drive that memory back into its deep, dark corner in his mind.

Did I Really Say That?

From time to time, we all say things that don't quite come out the way we mean. Most of the time, we hope that no one will notice the error of our ways. I'm not that lucky. I have had some rather spectacular disasters develop right before my eyes, when I failed to consider the possible interpretations of something I say.

Comedian Bill Engvall has a great routine in which he says we should be able to give people a sign that says, "I'm stupid," when they ask or say something totally out to lunch. He has dozens of examples of times when he'd like to just say, "Here's your sign."

I probably should have received my full share of signs over the years. I know I definitely should have gotten one a while back, when I stopped at the border coming home to Canada from Washington State. I cross that border frequently, and I'm pretty used to the questions that customs officers ask. Usually, all they want to know is the length of time that I spent in America and what goodies I might have picked up while I was there. I answer those questions honestly, because I don't want the guards on either side of the border to have a reason to say that I can't go across any more.

On the day in question, I had stopped a gas station. They had a certain brand of soft drink on sale, so I picked up a case. When I got to the border, I was asked the usual questions, and I answered them without really putting my brain in gear before opening my mouth. My reply wasn't just out to lunch. It was out to lunch, dinner, and the next morning's breakfast.

"I just went down for a couple of hours for a meeting and I picked up some Coke® on my way back," I said.

Apparently, that didn't immediately bring soft drink brands to the customs officer's mind. He thought of a different kind of coke. He wasn't thinking about solid mineral fuels, either. I might just as well have said that I was transporting the entire agricultural production of Columbia in my trunk.

I knew right away that I was going to be spending some time watching them check out all of the nooks and crannies in my car. There was no point trying to tell them that I wasn't a long-haired, bearded drug smuggler, just a long-haired, bearded soda drinker.

I'm just as guilty. In fact, I quite enjoy making the most of it when someone says something without thinking it through before opening their mouth. It's a habit that had my family in constant fear of what they might say that could end up in a column. Just to ensure them that their fears are not just paranoia, and despite the fact that the column ended four years ago, I'll tell you about a conversation I had with my wife the other day.

A news report the night before showed police in Los Angeles arresting a larger than life version of Sesame Street's Elmo, along with Batman and another character. I didn't hear what the whole story was, and it captured my curiosity. The next morning, I commented, quite innocently, that I still didn't know why Elmo was arrested.

Diane answered, momentarily forgetting that she has been married to a professional smartass for the past thirty-eight years, "They were just actors."

"Oh, thank goodness, "I responded. "I thought they were arresting the real Elmo. Was Batman there to help the police or was he a fake, too?"

I desperately wanted to say, "Here's your sign,' but I have a policy against using other writers' material. I also desperately wanted to avoid being hit by whatever she had in her hand at the time.

It can be hard, having to watch what I say to avoid confusing someone else. For that matter, I get into enough trouble by confusing myself. It's also hard not to enjoy the opportunities that Diane presents when she slips up.

Of course, it's even harder sleeping on the couch.

Flight Delays Of Mice And Men

I spent part of a day planning flights in and out of New York City. Between the three main airports there are a few hundred too many options to consider.

I've learned to avoid one airline, because I think every one of their flights requires a stopover in Houston. I have nothing against Houston. I just don't think I need to go there to fly from San Francisco to Los Angeles. I'm sure any of their flights to New York will take a side trip to the Gulf of Mexico, just for the heck of it.

Naturally, whenever you are planning flights these days, the specter of air terror raises its ugly head. With that in mind, I suppose I should have expected that several news stories would cross my desk about airline horrors as soon as I bought my ticket.

I feel reasonably confident in the airport security people. From what I've seen they are more than capable of saving me from a grandmother carrying a large bottle of shampoo in her carry-on luggage. On the other hand, they seem to have a tendency of letting one group slip through security with less than an adequate degree of scrutiny. In my experience, these people cause more terror in the minds of passengers than anyone else.

Of course, I'm talking about the pilots.

Two pilots, who were featured in news items, made me glad I rarely use their airlines. Airport security could have done a lot better job of preventing them from getting too close to the cockpits.

A Northwest pilot had to be removed from his plane after he held a long and loud cellular phone conversation filled with obscenities, while the passengers were boarding.

Oh sure, we've all had bad days at the office, and most of us have had the desire to let someone know our true feelings with a few well-placed explicative descriptions of what they should do with themselves, where, and how often they should do it. Apparently, the pilot in question didn't have the common sense to have his conversation out of the earshot of those not involved.

The Las Vegas police were called to remove him from the plane after he cursed out a passenger who suggested he tone it down a bit. It's not the sort of behavior that is going to get him included on the airline's 'Meet The Shining Stars of Northwest' web page.

Airport security also let a Virgin Atlantic pilot pass through without delay, even though he smelled of alcohol. Another airport worker noticed and alerted authorities. The airline reinstated that pilot. He hadn't been drinking at all. His low carbohydrate diet caused him to smell of alcohol. I don't know about you, but I plan on filing that excuse away for future use.

"No I haven't been drinking, Officer. I'm on a low carbohydrate diet. It just makes my breath smell like the downwind side of a distillery"

There have been several reports in recent years about inebriated pilots. I have to wonder about the one who pulled out onto the runway my plane was approaching in Washington, DC a few years ago. It's probably a pretty safe bet that my pilot used a few well-placed obscenities, when he had to abort our landing.

I know I did.

It wasn't the pilots who caused an air security problem in Vietnam a few years ago. A friend of mine, who did a lot of flying in Vietnam in the late Sixties, says he never once felt secure, but that's another story. The Boeing aircraft in this case was a 777, not an F-104 fighter jet.

Passengers were delayed for over four hours after the plane was evacuated and all the luggage was removed in Hanoi. They weren't looking for bombs. Apparently, someone had boarded the flight in Danang with a companion not listed on the flight manifest. The stowaway, a white mouse, got loose on the plane causing the delay,

I'm on a pretty tight schedule for my flight to New York. I'd appreciate it if no one lets a mouse loose on the plane. I'd also like the airline to make sure the pilot is in a good mood and has had his full daily intake of carbohydrates before heading to the airport.

And let's skip the side trips to Houston.

Something A Little Nuts For Your Dog

It probably goes without saying that I love my dog. There is not much I wouldn't do for her, and there are those who think I spoil her. OK, so she's the only dog I am aware of that has over twenty stuffed animals in her toy bin, but she gets so much enjoyment carrying them around the house, it's hard to pass up bringing another one into the house for her.

Tara also has some heavy rubber balls that she throws around the room. They bounce in odd and unexpected directions when she shakes her head and lets them fly. I also bounce in some unexpected directions when one lands in my crotch. She tends to throw them at me if she thinks she hasn't been getting enough attention. Believe me; nothing can grab your attention away from the newspaper or a television program than a hard rubber toy hitting you in that particular region.

One of the requirements when we got Tara to have her trained as my disability service dog was that she be spayed. Bob Barker would be so pleased. She has never shown any adverse effects or psychoses resulting from her inability to breed. Our former dog, Nipper, also known as the dumbest dog to ever get lost on a single flight of stairs, developed some odd sexual desires after her trip to the vet's. For the rest of her life she would steal cushions and pillows and try to mate with them. I suppose better that than a guest's leg.

Apparently, there is a concern that some male dogs are feeling a bit light in the nether regions after they are neutered. I suppose it might be a bit embarrassing for them to stop by the hydrant and have other dogs discover the truth during a joint consensual sniffing.

You just had to know that someone, somewhere, somehow would come up with a solution. That man was Gregg A. Miller of Independence, Missouri. In 1995, after he had his bloodhound neutered, he came up with the idea for Neuticles®, artificial testicles for dogs. According the website of CTI Corporation (Canine Testicular Implantation), over 100,000 dogs worldwide have been the proud recipients of artificial testicles.

These aren't any cheap, one-size-fits-all enhancements. Depending on the model you chose for your dog, there are as many as eight different sizes. They come in the original rigid model, or in what the company calls 'Natural Soft.' They range from petite, for dogs between one and three pounds all the way up to XX-Large for dogs up to 190 pounds.

By now, you all know how my mind works. You've probably already figured out that I am sitting here considering the possibility of XX-Large Neuticles® on some little piece of shih tzu. It might have difficulty chasing a ball, but you can bet it would be the cock of the walk down at the off-leash park.

They aren't just for dogs anymore. The company now makes artificial testicles for horses and bulls. While the petite canine version is less than an half an inch long, the large equine and bull version is 5.75" in length.

There are even feline versions for those people who don't mind sharing their home with a litter box. We've had cats over the years, and thankfully don't anymore, but there was one who stood out in that department. Dusty (a name he got from the only thing found inside his skull) only had one real purpose in my mind. That was the sheer entertainment value of watching people's expressions if they saw him walking away. You could say that he was particularly well endowed, and he walked proudly, with his tail held high. What made him particularly entertaining was his ability to rotate his testicles in opposite directions as he walked; clockwise on the right and counter clockwise on the left. It was truly a sight to behold.

Had he ever lost the equipment necessary for that little trick, I might have considered digging deep into my pockets for the $229 to replace them. Heck, I might have even been willing to go completely nuts and drop $649 for the large bull versions for him to rotate.

Now, *that* would have been entertaining.

Are You Being Serviced?

One of the great oxymorons in our language is 'customer service.' At least it is if you think it means that you, as a customer, might get some service. Lately, it seems to fit more with the definition of service used by a cattle farming friend of mine. He talks about having his bull service his cows. As customers, we seem to be getting that kind of servicing more often than the sort we might hope for or expect.

It's certainly been the case with the wireless telephone company I have been dealing with (and will soon no longer be dealing with.) Their customer service is the main reason I will be switching to another supplier. After trying to deal with them on a number of occasions, and looking at the bill I get from them each month, I really think I am being serviced in the cattle sense of the word.

I called them a couple of months ago. As with so many companies lately, the customer service number is now being answered by a talking computer with a snotty attitude. It's enough to make you think the premise behind those Terminator movies might have been right.

These talking computers are used for one of two purposes. Naturally, they cut the cost of operations. That leaves more money for bonuses for the senior executives. More importantly, they are put in place for the simple purpose of frustrating any customer silly enough to call in for customer service. After a couple of minutes you either hang up, or forget why you called in the first place. It saves the company from having to solve any problem you might be having.

I'm convinced that my wireless provider hired Hal, the computer from *2001: A Space Odyssey*. It did such a good job messing with Dave's mind, that it would be the perfect candidate.

When I called, the disembodied voice asked for my account information. It would be fine if it stopped there, but like some three-year-old who picked up a telephone, it wants to know why you called.

"I want to talk to customer service," I said.

"I didn't quite catch that, I think you said you wanted to speak to technical support. Is that correct? Just say 'yes' or 'no'."

"No."

"OK, what do you need technical support for? Is your wireless telephone, home phone, television service, or internet?"

After I several excruciating minutes of this I said, "Just open the freaking pod bay doors, Hal."

"I didn't quite catch that. I think you said you were calling about your internet. Is that correct?"

I remembered that you could sometimes bypass these talking computers by pushing zero. When I did that, good old Hal came back and said, "Before I pass you to an agent, I just have a few more questions."

"Noooooooooooooooooooooooooo!"

He seemed to get that message. I was put on hold for the next available operator. Eighteen minutes later, 'the next available operator' reluctantly answered the phone.

This morning I got an email telling me that my current bill was available to be viewed on the internet. It also said "We're pleased to announce that we've made some exciting improvements to our online billing service to make it easier, faster, and more convenient for you to use."

I signed onto their website, and clicked the button to see my bill. It took me to a webpage that was blank, except for the message, "Microsoft VBScript compilation error "800a0411" Name redefined /Customercare/OnlineBilling/xtOnlineBillingConstants.asp,line 6 const LOG_TO_FILE = false should be set to false on production."

Somehow that just didn't feel exciting, easier, faster, or more convenient. To avoid talking to the computer again, I sent them an email about the problem.

Their reply said I should call their online service department to have them troubleshoot the problem. Clearly, the problem is at their end of the connection, and the person who wrote the reply could have spoken to the online service department, especially since she signed the email, "Vanessa S., Online Customer Service." She just wanted me to talk to Hal again.

It helped me make my decision. I'm switching providers, and this one can, in the cattle farmer's terminology, go service themselves.

Prison Reform Starts At The Bottom

It must be a horrible life for prisoners these days. We've all heard the horror stories from detention centers in Iraq and Afghanistan, but what about poor misguided robbers, murderers, and jaywalkers here in North America?

There are several prisons within a few miles of where I live. I can't imagine the hardships faced by the inmates. Clearly, the threat of prison time at one of these places should be deterrent enough for people considering a life of crime. Can you imagine the sheer degradation that new prisoners sent to Ferndale Prison in Mission, BC must feel when they discover that the golf course is just a nine-hole? How about the poor murderer who had to ship his own horse to the facility? I'll bet that is enough to make him think twice before he kills his next wife.

Parents have often used the hardship of prison as an example to help them keep their children on the straight and narrow. I wish I had known about the Hutchinson Correctional Facility in Kansas when my sons were young and impressionable. I might have tried to enforce the rules around here a little bit more along the lines of how they do it there.

Things would have flowed a lot better if I had.

A news item crossed my desk about Hutchinson. Apparently, inmates there are now limited to just one roll of toilet paper per week. The article didn't say if they get the kind with a couple hundred sheets or if they are supplied with the big thousand-sheet size.

It doesn't really matter. I could have used a rule like that. It would have resulted in a lot less wear and tear on our toilet plungers. I think we single-handedly kept a couple of paper mills in operation during the Nineties, just to keep up with my sons' consumption. Had the article about Hutchinson appeared back then I would have laminated a copy and hung it beside the toilet. It might not have cut down on their paper use, but it would have been positive reinforcement for living by the rules.

The reduction in toilet paper allotment understandably has prisoners in a crappier mood than usual, but prison officials say that they expect to save $600 a month by limiting the number of rolls of toilet paper. They also plan to limit soap and toothpaste for even greater savings. Those who feel the need for more will have to purchase their own at the prison canteen. A four-roll pack of Charmin® costs them $2.70.

I wonder if they prefer the scented or the one with lotion injected into the sheets.

Ever since they retired old Mr. Whipple, Proctor and Gamble have been using animated bears to promote the concept that even the bears that poop in the woods prefer Charmin®. I wonder if they'll launch an ad just for the prisoners, with the bears wearing stripes and leg irons. They could even bring back a shotgun-toting Mr. Whipple telling prisoners on a chain gang not to squeeze the Charmin® in the portable outhouse.

There is a concern that toilet paper will become a new form of currency at Hutchinson. Kansas Department of Corrections spokeswoman Frances Breyne admits that anything that is restricted automatically becomes a means of dealing and trading. I suppose different brands could represent different denominations.

You sure wouldn't want to take an old crumpled up bill in your change.

Forget files. Can you imagine the size of the cake the prisoners' wives are going to have to bake to conceal a 36-roll warehouse club package of toilet paper? Fox Broadcasting could develop a spin-off to

Prison Break, in which a character gets the blueprints to a prison, printed on a roll of contraband toilet tissue, brought in by his brother. It would probably be easier to read than a tattoo, just not as waterproof.

If the officials at Hutchinson really want to make prison life less comfortable, they could buy the toilet paper that's dispensed a single sheet at a time at those roadside rest stops. After all, it's rough, it's tough, and it sure won't take any crap from me.

...or anyone else.

Canada: Where Consenting Numismatics Go To Party

A couple of years ago, my country unveiled a new coin. I have boycotted it. I will never accept one in change. I won't even try to flip one to settle a dispute. Enough is enough. My pockets just won't handle the increased wear and tear.

For my American readers I should point out that, in Canada, we do not have one or two-dollar bills. The dollar bill disappeared in 1987, replaced by a brass-colored coin, called the loonie. There is a

Canadian loon on the tails side. The head side features the matriarch of the world's most famous dysfunctional family, Elizabeth the Second. I've never been sure which loon gave the coin its name.

Our two-dollar bill went the way of the one in 1996. Its replacement has since become known as a twoonie, although I always thought that it would have been better to call it a doubloon. In keeping with the animal motif, there is a polar bear on the tails side. As far as I know, it is still the only coin ever made with a portrait of the Queen with a bear behind.

As a result, if your purchases total $5.01, all of your change from a ten will be in the form of coins. At the end of a day of shopping, men start walking a bit lopsided because of the weight in their pockets. Purse snatchers have been known to get hernias, trying to grab a purse filled with small change.

I've always preferred paper money, especially my country's. Each of our remaining bills is a different color, making them easy to sort in your wallet, and a great deterrent to crime. With blue fives, purple tens, green twenties, and pink fifties, any would-be money launderer would have to do too many separate loads to make it worth his while.

Somewhere, deep in the bowels of the Canadian government, in the place where they keep the brain trust, someone came up with the idea of adding another coin to our currency. This time, instead of replacing one of our bills, they decided that we need an entirely new denomination. I might have gone along with the idea, if they issued a $1.12 coin so I could make my purchases and pay my sales tax at the same time.

Of course, that would have made too much sense.

Apparently, the impetus for issuing this new coin comes, not from some clear need for it, but because we want to show the world that we are bigger and better than Austria, the current world leader in silly coin production. As a result, Canadians can now pocket a $1-million coin.

Pocket may not be the appropriate word. The coin is 20 inches in diameter, 1 inch thick, and weighs roughly 220 pounds. So take that Austria. Your puny little alternative that is in the current Guinness Book Of Records as the world's largest coin is a measly 70 pounds. I may be big for my age, but even my pockets would need major alterations to carry either one of them around.

I wonder if they will have to alter vending machines to give change for a million.

I think I know where Canada got the idea. In 2004, a woman tried to pass a $1-million bill in a Wal-Mart store in Covington, Georgia. The cashier didn't have the $998,328.45 necessary to make change, so she called her manager. The manager thought it just might be counterfeit, so the police were called. They found two similar bills in her purse. I guess she hadn't been to Booze-R-Us yet.

I might have to wonder about the intelligence of the shoppers and staff of that Walmart, if one thought her husband had really given her a million-dollar bill, and the others were unsure what to do about making change. I "might" but then again, I have ventured into a Walmart on a couple of occasions.

Million-dollar coins and bills may not be as silly as they appear at first glance. A hundred years ago, the thought of a fifty or hundred-dollar bill might have seemed unreal for the average person. Today, it's just the down payment on a tank of gas for an SUV.

Canada may not be near the top of the most powerful nation on the planet lists. Our official motto translates to "Hey! Hey! We're number 60! Watch your step 59!" When it comes to making big honking coins though, we're number one.

You just can't get any loonier than us.

Pop Goes The Tenor

One look at the song list in my iPod will tell you that my musical tastes are somewhat varied, or as one person said, "It looks like it was put together by someone with a severe multiple personality disorder."

I've said it before, and I'll say it again. I do not have a multiple personality disorder…

…and neither do I.

You will find Jimi Hendrix mixed in with Garth Brooks, the Dixie Chicks are right behind Dire Straits, along with Tony Bennett, Van Morrison, and enough Dylan to keep you mumbling along with him for two or three days. Every Beatles song is there, as is Joni

Mitchell's entire discography. There are folksongs from the people I worked with in coffee houses in the late Sixties and early Seventies such as Bruce Cockburn and new folk material by my musical partner in crime, Greg Greenway.

There's rock, folk, and country. Sweet sounds from Joni Mitchell are thrown in with the harder sounds of The Who and ZZ Top. The early rock era is covered by groups such as The Four Seasons and The Beach Boys. Sheryl Crow and U2 represent more current music.

When the mood strikes me and there's a drop of the pure in my glass, there are several dozen Irish drinking songs to set the mood for a good old fashioned Irish hangover in the making.

The songs of the late Phil Ochs are there for the times I feel nostalgic for the days of the civil rights movement. More poetry than lyrics, his songs got me in trouble in one high school English class, and helped me pass another. I used his Here's To The State of Mississippi in a speech in grade ten. A note went home to my parents that I was not to bring my radical political views to class in the future. In grade twelve, I had to recite a poem by heart. Ochs had put Alfred Noyes poem, The Highwayman, to music, and made it easy for me to recite the words while hearing the song in my head.

My iPod contains the soundtrack of my life. Shelves of CDs are now crammed into a little box that fits into my shirt pocket. Frankly, it's a bit disturbing to think that my whole musical life can fit into something that small. On the other hand, I'm thankful, because it was getting difficult to carry around a couple hundred CD's and a stereo system wherever I went.

That soundtrack does not include opera. I often wondered how my father could complain that he couldn't understand a word that was said in any of the songs I listened to, and yet he could sit through an opera diva on the Ed Sullivan Show making noises as if someone had just set her toenails on fire.

A couple of weeks ago, Diane and I were given tickets to see 'pop opera.' I had no idea what that was. From what I learned at the concert, it involves singing a medley of Bee Gees, Everly Brothers, and Moody Blues songs in an operatic fashion.

And in Italian.

The four singers looked like they had stepped off the cover of a romance novel with a title like "He Hit Her High Note." I had never heard of them, but apparently enough people to fill a 16,000-seat NHL arena had.

The audience was predominantly female. Apparently, most of them, and a few of the men (not that there's anything wrong with that) wanted the singers to hit their personal high notes. There was screaming whenever they moved. At virtually every pause someone shouted "I love you." The front row was filled with women waving Italian flags in time with the music. Near the end of the show hundreds of women, many looking old enough to have given birth to any or all of the singers, rushed the stage.

Well, OK, maybe rushed wasn't the right word. Most waddled.

It served to put the concept of pop opera into perspective. Unlike the more stereotypical opera performances, pop opera "ain't over until the fat lady throws her panties onto the stage."

Does An Author Poop In The Woods? ...Almost

When I was a child there was a radio program that came on during the lunch hour featuring stories and songs for young children. The theme music for the show was The Teddy Bears' Picnic.

"If you go out in the woods today, you're sure of a big surprise..."

I went out in the woods the other day, and yes, I got a big surprise; one I hope that won't be repeated anytime soon. Frankly, I blame my doctor and his "get more exercise" mantra for the surprise ending to my sojourn into the forest.

I've often heard about a trail in the mountains north of my place that is groomed to make it accessible for the disabled. I happened to be driving past it recently, on a day that I had some time to kill. Hearing my doctor's words, I decided to give it a try. I grabbed my camera, and put Tara, my assistance dog, into her harness. Together we set out from the parking lot, and were soon totally secluded from the sounds of the highway.

The walk was pleasant. The trail was better than I expected it to be. The forest was filled with new spring growth. Birds were singing, and all along the way I could hear the sound of a river rushing toward a waterfall. When we reached the end of the trail, we discovered that there was a large observation platform looking out over the waterfall as it dropped a couple of hundred feet into a small canyon.

When Tara and I started back toward the car we were walking into the wind. It was cool, but not unpleasant. We took our time, partially because I was enjoying the scenery, and partially because Tara had to sniff every tree, rock, and blade of grass just in case some other dog might have left her a pee-mail message.

Three quarters of the way back to the car I heard a rustling in the brush. The source of that sound gave everyone involved 'a big surprise.' Tara didn't expect what we saw, I was certainly unprepared for what we saw, and I am pretty sure the very large black bear that stepped out of the woods and onto the trail about twenty-five feet ahead of us was completely unprepared to see us.

This was most assuredly not one of the friendly teddy bears that were the subject of the song from so many years ago. It didn't look like the sort of animal that would sit around in a group eating finger sandwiches.

Fingers maybe, but only if it has room after eating your other body parts.

Part of Tara's training involves stepping between me and anything that she considers dangerous. In the past that has been largely limited to other dogs, the occasional coyote, and a couple of very startled Jehovah Witnesses. True to her duty, she planted herself between the bear and me, but I don't think she was all that crazy about the idea. Her tail, which is normally wagging, was tucked so far between her legs that she probably could have tickled her own chin with its tip.

The bear looked at us and grunted loudly. I waved one of my crutches in the air and shouted. I don't think I frightened the bear, but now that I think of how I must have looked, it probably thought I was nuts. Either way, it decided that it didn't want to have anything to do with me, despite nuts being a big part of a bear's diet. It slowly sauntered back into the forest.

Knowing that people might not believe me, I quickly took a couple of pictures. The bear turned when the shutter clicked and grunted again. I got the message it was trying to convey – "No pictures."

I was right about needing photographic evidence. When I told the story to a friend, he gave me an incredulous look. It was just as I suspected. He was having difficulty believing that I'd actually go out and willingly do something to get some exercise.

I hardly believe it myself.

Proof That The End Is Near

It has to be a sure sign of the apocalypse approaching at warp speed. Life on Earth is doomed. Civilization is crumbling around us. Frankly, I'm worried about this. It's not war that has me spooked. Terrorism is bad, but this is worse. Religious fanaticism from all sides might bring on the end, but this will surely bring it sooner.

Some idiot tried to put bingo on prime-time TV.

Oh sure, bingo has been around the tube on and off over the years, but that has usually been in advertising for a local grocery store or as a fundraiser for a service club. Forget about those minor little aberrations. It is truly a sign of our impending demise when they try to make bingo a prime time event.

I thought TV was going downhill when shows started running paternity tests for grade-school dropouts and calling it entertainment. The whole 'reality-TV' wave has crashed down on intelligently written programming like a tsunami hitting *Survivor's* latest island. This kind of programming has already been apocalyptic for the careers of several of my friends in the business. Who needs writers and actors, when you can put a bunch of mindless gold diggers into a rented mansion vying for an engagement ring and convince enough mindless viewers that it's 'must-see TV.'

The powers that be in the network boardrooms have decided to cancel well written programs, no doubt to replace them with more unreal reality.

But bingo? Yep. The end is near.

Maybe I have a deep psychological aversion to bingo. One of the very first columns I wrote, when I started back in 1994 was about my dislike for bingo. At the time, my sons were attending a Catholic elementary school (something they still have not forgiven their mother and me for.) If you didn't show up and work at the parish bingo night once a month, your children's tuition doubled for that month.

It was church sanctioned extortion. Apparently, one of the biblical codes indicates that if you take the first letter of certain verses, you will get, "Thou shalt force your parishioners to endure smoky bingo halls." It's right there in the Bible.

As I wrote at the time, very few actually played bingo. As I understand the rules of the game, you are supposed to cover the numbers the caller announces and then shout, "Bingo!" The vast majority played 'Aw-sh…' In Aw-sh… you don't cover the numbers announced, and when someone else in the room shouts "Bingo," you mutter "Aw-sh…" Out of respect for the church hall, you don't complete that phrase with the letters 'i' and 't'.

For eight years, I had to endure the monthly bingo ritual. It was bad for my health. At the time, no one considered the harm of second hand smoke. By the end of the night the room looked like it was the smoldering remnants of a three-alarm blaze. The smoke in the room was so thick, even people with a two pack a day habit, had to take breaks to get some fresh air.

I felt guilty after each time I had to work the bingo hall. Seeing people that I knew could little afford it, buying wads of bingo cards in the hopes of winning a $25.00 jackpot, was not my idea of a responsible way to raise money for the school. I tried to institute an alternative fundraiser that over two years brought in close to $50,000.00 for the school, but the administrators simply saw that as augmenting the bingo income. They couldn't break free of the money the games brought in each week.

Bingo – the crack cocaine of parochial school treasurers.

So now bingo has come to prime time TV. I suppose it's only a natural progression down our path to destruction. After all, poker is now a spectator event on the sports channels. I happened across it one night when I was channel surfing. When I did, I experienced an unpleasant sensation, even though I quickly changed the channel. I could have sworn the room suddenly smelled of stale tobacco and Aw-sh... players.

The sounds and smells of the approaching apocalypse.

And I Thought I Could Eat

A read a news report about a woman who ate 26 hot dogs in twelve minutes. My first reaction to this story was, "Why?"

The answer, of course, is that she was participating in an event sanctioned by Major League Eating (MLE).

This is one of those cases that makes me want to quote my friend Dave Barry, who would often say "I'm not making this up" in his column, but because I don't want to use a line he used so frequently, I will just say I'm not screwing with your head. There is an actual sports league called Major League Eating.

According to the online encyclopedia, Wikipedia, it is the International Federation of Competitive Eating brand that designates all top-level competitive eaters, eating events, television specials, and merchandise.

At last, a sport for that husky kid who always got picked last for baseball.

Or is it? Juliet Lee, the Chinese émigré who downed 26 wieners and buns on June 16, 2007 weighed in at just 107 pounds. The average Nathan's hot dog weighs 3-1/2 ounces. The bun adds roughly another 1-1/2 ounces. That means she added over eight pounds to her body weight in twelve minutes. Second place went to a 359-pound man who was only able to consume 15-1/2. The 360-pound third place finisher only managed ten.

You might be tempted, as I was, to doubt that competitive eating is really a sport. I can assure you that it is. If it wasn't would ESPN be televising the events? There's the thrill of victory and the foul taste of defeat (probably for several hours afterward.) It has to rank right up there in excitement with watching their broadcast of the Scripps Howard Spelling Bee. Forget baseball, football, and hockey. ESPN brings us competitive eating and some kid spelling "serrefine." I can hardly handle the excitement, but then I'm Canadian and we watch curling.

I Googled the International Federation of Competitive Eating's website. The page I was taken to was a news report about a horseshoe eating contest. My first thought was that you would never be able to go through airport security on your way home from the contest, but you would certainly boost your iron intake.

Thankfully, they were talking about Illinois horseshoes. They do not go on equestrian hooves. Apparently, and my readers in Illinois, please back me up on this, an Illinois horseshoe is two pieces of toast stuffed with ham, French fries, and cheese sauce. I can hear my arteries clogging just thinking about them. The current MLE record holder, one Joey Chestnut, who is seeded number two in the league's competitive eater rankings, ate 6 pounds, 5 ounces of them in twelve minutes.

The event that Ms. Lee won, was just one of the preliminary rounds leading up to Nathan's Famous July Fourth International Hot Dog Eating Contest, held in Coney Island, N.Y. She'll be up against some serious competition there. Twenty-six hot dogs is less than half of the current MLE hot dog eating record, also held by the same Joey Chestnut, at 59-1/2 in twelve minutes. That's over fifteen pounds.

I've cooked smaller turkeys.

Susan McQuillan, a New York registered dietitian, calculated that Mr. Chestnut took in 16,532 calories from the record hot dog binge. They represented 535% of the daily recommended cholesterol intake, 1525% of the recommended daily sodium, and 1657% of the daily fat consumption recommendation.

I'm not a particularly religious person, but I seem to recall the irony of a rotund Sunday school teacher telling the class that the Bible calls gluttony one of the seven deadly sins. I would imagine that consuming 1657% of the recommended daily fat intake might very well be one of the ways to make it deadly.

We all know what goes up must come down, and what goes in must come out. I have to wonder how many minutes it took Ms. Lee to 'eliminate' those 26 hot dogs the next day, and how painful a process that was. At least she wasn't trying to beat the record for eating 8.4 pounds of baked beans in two minutes, forty-seven seconds.

They'd need a HAZMAT team to handle that.

It Ain't Me, Babe

I have been accused of a lot of strange things, but this is definitely a first.

When I turned on my computer this morning, I sat, not so patiently, watching the email program import all of the messages that had been sent to me overnight. The emails are automatically sorted into folders that someone-who-knows-how-these-things-work set up to keep me organized.

Someone-who-knows-how-these-things-work doesn't realize that using the term, 'organized,' and my name in the same sentence is an oxymoron.

Most of my emails go directly into the folder that is reserved for offers to sell me Viagra and other "cheap Canadian pharmaceuticals," requests to help someone get millions of dollars out of Nigeria, and products guaranteed to make me "explode in bed." I'm not sure why someone-who-knows-how-these-things-work doesn't just make the program immediately delete these emails. I really don't want to read any of them because:

As a Canadian, I can get cheap Canadian pharmaceuticals at the drug store around the corner.

I don't need the money from Nigeria, because I have already won seventeen lotteries I didn't even know I entered, and I expect my huge payouts to arrive anytime soon.

I'm flying to Scotland in two weeks, and I don't really want to think about any kind of explosions right now, thank you very much.

One of those folders collects all of the emails that tell me when my name has been used in a news story or on a website somewhere. The main purpose of these emails is to see how the promotional activities for my books are succeeding. As I sat watching this morning's emails coming in, a pattern started to emerge. There seemed to be an awful lot of emails going into the 'your name has been used folder.' By the time it stopped, there were sixteen new messages. Four more came in while I've been writing this story.

I've learned not to get too excited about these emails. While they are often confirmation that the publicity efforts are working, they can occasionally be sent in error. If anyone who shares my name, or for that matter, if anyone named Gordon in Kirkland,

WA or Kirkland Lake, ON makes the news, I hear about it.

I get regular updates about the activities of Gordon Kirkland, who is an administrator in the Athletics Department at Catawba College in North Carolina. I've spoken with that Gordon Kirkland, and he'd like you to know that there will be a reunion of Catawba College baseball players next year.

Go Indians.

His father, another Gordon Kirkland, also occasionally pops up in my emails. Despite having passed away some time ago, the fact that he is a member of North Carolina's Sports Hall of Fame deserves a mention from time to time.

There is another author by the name of Gordon Kirkland. Anyone who checks an online bookstore for my books will also be shown his book, Advances in the Biology of Shrews. I think it's about small furry rodents, not shrews in the Shakespearean sense.

Today's emails came from newspapers, radio stations, television stations, and online wire services. Naturally, I was curious to see just what had suddenly piqued the media's interest in me. I opened one of the emails and read the headline:

Pregnant Teen, Boyfriend Murder Parents

I was certain that it wasn't about me, because you'd think I might remember something about that sort of thing. Still, seeing that headline is like spotting a car wreck on the highway. I had to look.

Apparently, a fifteen-year-old girl and her twenty-one-year-old boyfriend killed the girl's father and stepmother because they didn't approve of their relationship. (Gee. I wonder why.) They have a friend named Gordon Kirkland. He has also been charged with first-degree murder because he knew about their plans.

Thanks a bunch, Gordo.

Online telephone directories show that there are almost twenty Gordon Kirklands spread around the United States and Canada. I'd like to ask them all a favor. It's one thing to plan a baseball reunion, write a book about rodents, or play in US National Doubles Racquetball Championships, but if you want to go around murdering people, please use a pseudonym.

Maybe 'Scooter' Something.

A Weird World Of Sports

It's that time of the year we all look forward to. Major sporting events are turning up wherever you look. It's like a cafeteria of excuses to avoid household chores. There's the Major League Baseball All Star Game, dozens of golf tournaments, and so very much more.

It's that 'so very much more' that has me wondering if we've all gone a bit nuts.

East Dublin, GA hosts the annual Redneck Games each July. It all started in 1996 as a way of attracting tourists who might otherwise have had to sit through the Olympic Games in Atlanta that year. Why watch a bunch of European rhythmic gymnasts when you can enjoy events like the Mud Pit Belly Flop? Other events in the Redneck Games include a form of horseshoes using toilet seats, bobbing for pigs' feet, and watermelon seed spitting.

Before my Canadian readers get too smug about American rednecks, there is a Canadian version of the Redneck Games held in Minto, Ontario. Yee-haw, eh?

I'm thinking I should start training for next year's watermelon spitting event. It was certainly a big part of my upbringing, sitting across the table from my older brother and sister. They may have had better aims, but I certainly would have scored higher in artistic merit. I can still see my father, looking slightly cross-eyed as a watermelon seed slid down the front of his bifocals after one of my errant, although artistic, misfires.

For those who prefer more of a European flare to their sports viewing, there is always the running of the bulls in Pamplona, Spain to draw your attention away from the yard work.

This year the bulls gored 2 runners and crushed another seven as they charged down the narrow streets. I'm sure a good goring is every bit as exciting as a flaming wreck at a NASCAR race, but that's not the big news out of Pamplona this year.

A few women run side by side with men each year, but now a group of them want their own separate run. They don't want to be chased through the streets by a bunch of testosterone filled beasts. They get enough of that in the bars around town. Apparently, they would prefer to have an equally feminine group of adversaries pursuing them.

They want to call it The Running Of The Cows.

(You know, some jokes just write themselves...)

I'm not going to go where that leads me - at least not in public - because if I do, I will get flooded with hate mail, my editors will get flooded with mail about hating me, and my wife will hold it up as just one more piece of evidence that I am not as evolved as I claim to be.

I'll leave it to the Finns to bring male chauvinism to a new height in sports. Sonkajarvi, Finland was recently home to the 12th annual wife carrying competition, in which men must run and wade through a pool, carrying a woman on their backs. This is not your piggy-back race of old. In Sonkajarvi, the women hang upside-down with their legs wrapped around the men's necks as they try to cover the 250-metre course.

(I'm not going there, either, but I think the Kama Sutra may have.)

The current record is just over fifty-six seconds, but this year's winner was a full five seconds off that pace. The winners receive plasma televisions and the weight of their passenger in beer – a little over thirteen gallons this year. That may explain why the

Irish contestant carried the heaviest woman in the race, but only managed a 29th place finish.

It's also the time of year for the Tour de France bicycle race. Let's face it. The only reason most people watch the race each day is to see which steroid-filled rider will cause the biggest crash.

Between the muddy belly flops, Tour de France wrecks, NASCAR collisions, wife-carrying hernias, and Pamplona gorings, I'm glad I'm not a fan of any of those events. I'm anxiously waiting for hockey to return to my TV in about three months.

At least it isn't so violent.

Back In (And Out Of) The Saddle Again

Many years ago, I wrote a column about something I thought had ended with the accident that broke my spine. A misunderstanding on the part of some readers caused my editors to receive a great deal of mail from people who stopped reading after the first couple of paragraphs.

I wrote, "I miss the feel of hot, sweaty flesh, pounding rhythmically beneath me, and the sounds of heavy breathing and snorting as I arc up and down - at times barely able to avoid falling off. It's not that I experienced it very often, and, frankly, I wasn't all that good at it, but every time I did, I had a great time."

Had those dirty-minded readers continued on, they would have discovered in the following paragraph that I was talking about horseback riding.

In 2004 I released my second book, with a title that has been referred to as 'words to live by.' *Never Stand Behind A Loaded Horse* was launched amid much fanfare at a fundraiser for a disabled riding center. The book cover shows me standing at the back end of one of the horses from the riding center. I've often had to point out that I am the one on the left in the photograph. It's another horse's butt on the right.

A local newspaper sent a recent journalism school graduate to interview me, and photograph me on horseback. I told her how much riding meant to me, and quoted the English proverb saying, "The best thing for the inside of a man is the outside of a horse."

A few days later, the article appeared in the newspaper. To this day, I have not lived down being quoted as saying, "The best thing for the outside of a man is the inside of a horse."

I said it then, and I will say it again. I love horses, but it is strictly platonic.

When the opportunity to go for a trail ride with my son came up a couple of years ago, I decided to go for it.

I was given Yukon, a large Belgian draft horse. He was just slightly smaller than those Clydesdales you see pulling the Budweiser beer wagons. Despite being 6'4", getting onto the horse required that I stand on an elevated platform. Two people had to help pull my legs across the saddle, because that action required a movement that I no longer possess. It was, in all likelihood, the most ungraceful mounting in the history of riding.

We rode along a dusty trail outside Winthrop in eastern Washington. Aside from Brad and me, there were four other riders, two guides, and a trail boss along for the journey. I was the second rider in the line, behind one of the guides. Knowing full well how true the advice I gave calling my book Never Stand Behind A Loaded Horse, I kept about fifteen feet between my horse's head and the lead horse's butt.

I assumed it would be a leisurely ride. For the most part it was. Unfortunately, my horse did not like the dust kicked up by the lead horse billowing up his nose. After several minutes of walking through a brown cloud, he decided he'd had enough and broke into a gallop to get away from the dust. It took me a moment to remember how to ride at that pace. For the first couple strides, my butt came down as the saddle was came up. It felt like a couple vertebrae were going to shoot through the top of my skull.

After an hour and a half in the saddle, those who witnessed it told me that my dismount was even more entertaining than my mounting. All in all though, I had a great ride, certainly better than the rider immediately behind me. He probably wished old Yukon had been getting a bit more fiber in his diet.

That will teach him to ride so close to a loaded horse.

A Week With Scots and Scotch

I survived a week in Scotland, and I think Scotland survived a week with me, although I tried my best to single-handedly reduce their reserves of single malt scotch.

My wife and I were there, along with about eighty other couples from her firm, for a bit of corporate rest and relaxation. We didn't have time for much rest. The scotch helped, though.

Flying has never been my favorite activity, but Google's map program could not calculate driving directions from here to Scotland. Apparently, it has something to do with the large body of water in the middle of the route.

We flew into Heathrow and switched to a British Midland flight. If you're ever considering flying British Midland you should be aware of their motto, "You'll have to pay extra for that." The small bottle of water that any other airline hands out without charge was the equivalent of $3.00. Instead of an air marshal, I think the guy in the front seat was a mortgage broker, there in case someone might want to negotiate time payments for a bag of pretzels.

While much of England to the south of us was wading around in floodwaters, we remained relatively dry. The only real rain we saw was on the afternoon we toured a distillery. The guide pointed out that what was falling from the sky was just the raw material needed for the scotch they'd be bottling between 2017 and 2021.

The Scots know how to run a distillery tour. It was nothing like my experience at the Jack Daniels plant several years ago that ended in my great disappointment. It's in a dry county in Tennessee so they're only allowed to serve lemonade to the guests. At Glenkinchie, we moved quickly through the obligatory explanation of how they turned water and barley into scotch (truly a miracle of biblical proportions) and then entered the tasting room for a prolonged visit with several not-so-wee drams of the water of life.

I think I remember getting back on the bus.

We spent much of our time touring ancient castles. Edinburgh Castle was just a couple of blocks from our hotel. We also went to Sterling Castle, and Glamis Castle.

Glamis was particularly interesting for me because I enjoy Shakespeare. Macbeth was the fictional Thane of Glamis. It's said that Shakespeare was inspired by the rooms in the castle for the settings in the play. I was nearly inspired by the actions of Macbeth when our tour guide kept stepping in front of my camera.

You never see the apparition of a dagger when you really need one.

When I travel, I am always willing to try the local fare. That once left me thinking my back teeth had caught fire in a restaurant in Jakarta, but that's another story. In Scotland, the local fare includes the scotch that I so willingly sampled at every opportunity and the haggis and the black pudding that I didn't make me feel quite so willing.

At breakfast each morning there was haggis and black pudding on the buffet. I swallowed my pride, which it turned out was easier than swallowing the black pudding, and tried some. The haggis looked like a round sausage and tasted like lard. On the final night, we were served haggis at dinner that neither looked nor tasted like what I had seen at breakfast. I hate to admit it. It wasn't bad, but it could have been because the sauce they poured over it was made from scotch.

I'll put your mind at ease by telling you that I did not wear a kilt. A few of the men in our group rented them for the final dinner, and they cajoled me into paying a visit to the rental shop. Thankfully for all concerned, the tailor just looked at me and said, "Ach, noooooooooooo!" There was some reference to there not being enough tartan in all of Scotland to make a kilt my size.

At last, a wee benefit for being big for my age.

What Goes Up Must Come Down... Somewhere

Now I know why the Fifth Dimension sang about up, up, and away, but didn't mention down, down, and back.

We regained our senses and sold our condominium apartment and returned to a house a few years ago. We went through a prolonged period of home-selling experiences that could only happen to us. On the night we listed the apartment, the police discovered an old woman's body that had been in her bed for two weeks. The building had to be evacuated while exterminators dealt with the flies and other creepy-crawlies that had moved into her suite, and spread throughout the building. The building association nixed one sale because the buyer's dog was two inches too tall. We also dealt with several agents who did not rise to the level of their profession's standards. The one who broke the towel bar off the bathroom wall stands out, as does the one who called us to tell us, in no uncertain terms, what he thought of our agent because she had gone away for a weekend.

When all was said and done our agent asked us if we would like a certificate for a dinner at an upscale restaurant. A dinner out doesn't mean a whole lot to us. In fact, we're a little like my friend syndicated columnist Tracy Beckerman who says the best thing she knows how to make for dinner is reservations. We pointed out that the agent's company logo was its hot-air balloon, and asked if she could arrange for us to go for a flight sometime.

And that's where the up, up, and away comes in. On a warm summer evening, we took our maiden (and final) balloon flight. There were six passengers and the pilot, giving the whole adventure a Gilligan's Island feel.

I think I now know why hot-air balloons never caught on as a mode of transportation. It's that there's-no-way-to-steer-this-thing problem. Once aloft, you are basically at the mercy of the wind. The wind that night wasn't feeling particularly merciful.

Actually, it was a fantastic trip, although I do have videotaped evidence that my wife's comment on the ascension was, and I quote, "Woe-oh-ho-oh-eeeee-ooooo," followed by some fear induced giggling.

We rose to 2,200 feet and slowly sailed along heading east over farm fields and forests. The plan was that we would land at a farm a few miles from the small airport we left behind. That was the plan. It was a good plan. It just wasn't the wind's plan.

As we started to descend, the wind shifted and started pushing us north, away from the planned landing site. We skirted along at treetop height looking for another place to come down. First there was another farm field, but the pilot decided that hot air balloons and power lines didn't go well together. That thought gave me a new, heightened appreciation for his skills. We then aimed for a golf course that lets the balloon company land on its fairways when necessary. The only fairway on our trajectory was narrow and lined with tall trees. The pilot also thought hot air balloons probably shouldn't land in tall trees.

Did I mention how much I was starting to like this guy?

We sailed over a group of houses, just a couple of hundred feet over their rooftops. Dogs, as only dogs can do, ran in circles, loudly calling their masters out to see the thing overhead. One family waved to us. I shouted down to them, asking if we were anywhere near Kansas.

We finally aimed for the riding ring in a large equestrian center. We all crouched in the basket as it hit the ground for a brief instant. It lifted again, and came back down, this time tipping on its side. Naturally, I was on the side closest to the ground, with the weight of four other passengers pressing down on top of me.

Oh sure, I kissed the ground when I managed to extricate myself from the basket.

A week later two people died in a fire on board a hot air balloon that took off from the same small airfield we had used. It's enough to make me never want to see the inside of a balloon basket again, even if they give me the same pilot.

Still, I have to admit I liked his style, and that no landing in power lines policy.

I Hope My Characters Follow Instructions Better Than I Do

One of the most frequent questions my wife asks is, "What have you gotten yourself into now?" It's usually combined with her patented deer-in-the-headlights look. Occasionally, I even ask myself the same question, although I am not nearly as well practiced at the deer-in-the-headlights look. I've been asking myself that question quite a bit over the past few days.

In 2007, I let my name be put forward as a possible participant on a show on the Canadian TV channel, BookTelevision. The concept was tried for the first time the previous year. The show brought 12 Canadian writers together, and put them into a large bookstore for the Labor Day long weekend. In the 72 hours between midnight Friday and midnight Monday, they each had to complete a full novel.

Sleep was reserved for Tuesday.

They broadcast portions of the weekend live, and created a twelve-week TV series for later broadcast.

To make a long story short, I was selected for the cast of the 2007 show from a field of several hundred writers. That is what has put me into the aforementioned, 'what have you gotten yourself into now' frame of mind.

All of my previous books had been short humor stories that got their start in my newspaper column. They have all ranged from 600 to 1500 words. A novel, on the other hand is 60,000 to 150,000 words. It's almost uncharted territory for me.

When it became clear that I might be one of the twelve writers chosen to do the show, I had to come up with an idea. Thankfully, I have quite a few friends who are already novelists. They have offered me a great deal of encouragement over the years. One in particular, is Ridley Pearson. Ridley writes mystery novels that always seem to make their way onto the bestseller lists.

Several years ago, Ridley and I participated in a writing camp for high school seniors. For five days one hundred high school seniors lived and worked in cabins on an island in Puget Sound off Seattle. You could cut the sexual tension in those cabins with a knife, and that was just between the chaperones.

Our mutual friend, Dave Barry had just published his mystery novel, *Big Trouble*. Ridley said that I should follow Dave's lead and write a comedic mystery. I didn't think too much about it at the time, but it must have stayed in the back of my mind where the bats, moths, and other creatures reside. When the TV show came up, I remembered Ridley's suggestion.

I've learned a lot from Ridley and Dave, as well as from other friends like Jeffery Deaver and Nancy Warren. Apparently, novelists are supposed to be very organized. They also have to do something called research. They actually have to know something about what their characters are up to in their books.

Characters, on the other hand, are notorious for deciding to do or say things the novelist didn't consider when he or she started out.

The problem is that I am more like a character than a novelist. Diane says she's never sure what I will do or say, and, truth be known, neither am I. Apparently other people have noticed that about me, too. BookExpo-America named me one of their seven book industry characters. It came as no shock to my family that people think I am a character, and it probably isn't much of a stretch for the rest of you.

I had about three weeks to switch from character mode to novelist mode. As I created my characters, I tried to give them some general directions of what I expected them to do. Being a mystery novel, I'm expecting a certain amount of murder and mayhem. Even though *Fargo* is one of my favorite movies, I won't let my characters near a wood chipper.

I'm just not sure if they are listening to me.

When the time came to tape the show, I found myself spending the Labor Day weekend locked in a large bookstore with eleven other writers, under the watchful eyes of cameramen and television production people. Those who think my grasp of reality is tenuous at best, think it is rather odd that I would end up on a reality-TV series.

Most reality shows, seem to thrive on conflict. Some of the crew obviously hoped that we might be at each other's throats within a few minutes of the start of filming. Unfortunately for them, when you put a dozen writers into a room and give them a 72-hour deadline to finish a complete novel, you are going to find that their major conflict is with the clock, not each other.

We were provided with sleeping accommodations, which consisted of bunk beds in a room at the back of the store. Let me clarify that a bit. We were given child-size bunk beds. Being big for my age and a paraplegic, the top bunk was ruled out. It was all I could do to squeeze my body into the space allocated to the bottom bunk. As a result, I only spent a couple of hours there out of the whole weekend.

I knew, from watching the previous season's show that room was not off limits to the camera crew.

That year, a female contestant was shown, sleeping in her bunk, doing a pretty good impersonation of a gas-powered leaf blower. Because my wife has indicated in the past that I also snore, I resolved to do whatever was necessary to not be the star of this year's snore footage. I brought a supply of those strips that keep your nasal passages open. I just didn't expect the size of the beds would be my greatest ally in snore-prevention.

On the first night I slept for two hours. On the rest of the weekend I didn't even go to bed.

It wasn't really anything new for me. Each year, over the President's Day long weekend in February, I used to teach at the Southern California Writer's Conference in San Diego. Sleep is not a priority there, which is part of the reason why I say that event is too much fun to be legal in certain parts of North America.

Apparently sleep deprivation can do a real number on your synapses. At one point part way through the third night, I was sitting at my computer having a heated discussion with one of the characters from my book about how a scene should play out. I hadn't had a hallucinatory experience like that since sometime around 1969. To make matters worse, he was winning the argument.

By mid-morning on the final day, somewhere around the fifty-eighth hour, I had my story basically completed. Thankfully, they weren't expecting us to complete anything more than a good first draft. Turning it into a completed manuscript ready for publication would take a lot more work.

Of course, I would never get involved in something like this without expecting some sort of situation to arise that could only happen to me. Things seemed to be going along pretty smoothly through to the morning of Labor Day Monday. Obviously something had to give.

Because I hadn't gone to bed the night before, I went to the washroom to get cleaned up before the cast members who had actually slept managed to get up. Naturally, the camera crew followed me, but I managed to get everything but brushing my teeth done before they burst in on me. Television is not ready for full-frontal Kirkland.

When everyone else left the sleeping room, I slipped in, hoping to change quickly, without going through the contortions of trying to change under the covers. If I heard the door start to open I could yell out that whoever it was really didn't want to come in at that point.

Sleep deprivation makes you forget certain details, things like the fact that the window, which I was certain just looked out on the loading bay for the bookstore, didn't have curtains. Halfway through the changing process – in other words, all the way through the undressing process – I glanced at the window. It did face the loading bay, but on just the other side of that, there was the very full drive-through lane for a donut and coffee shop. A woman, who appeared to be well into her seventies, was staring back at me with her jaw dropped as far as it would go.

She probably still wakes up screaming in the middle of the night with that image racing through her subconscious.

Now, you probably will, too.

[**Author's note:** The story I wrote during the taping of the television series became my first novel, Crossbow.]

Typically Atypical

I have never been a member of any branch of the military. Therefore, I am not eligible for membership the various veterans' organizations. You'd think it would have protected me, but I still somehow managed to contract atypical pneumonia related to Legionnaire's Disease.

I have a penchant for getting things that are atypical. I didn't get the mumps as a kid, but I did miss six months of school in the eighth grade with Hepatitis A. I've written before about requiring anti-rabies vaccinations when I was eight. Typical people get the chicken pox. I got them too, but being atypical, I managed to do it not once, not twice, but on three separate occasions.

I'm told you aren't supposed to be able to do that. I just wish I hadn't gotten them that last time a meager six weeks after my wedding. The location of some of the sores was not something I could easily explain until after the doctor's diagnosis.

You try coming up with an explanation that would satisfy your new bride for bright red, blotchy sores appearing in and around your happy place. Thank goodness the doctor made house calls.

I had pneumonia once before, nearly thirty years ago. Naturally, it was atypical that time, as well. The lab tests confirmed that it was related to a condition called psittacosis, not one of your typical everyday ailments. Psittacosis is also known as parrot fever. When word of that diagnosis got out my so-called friends started delivering boxes of crackers, bags of sunflower seeds, and offers to save old newspapers for my cage floor.

But Legionnaire's Disease? Shouldn't you at least be able to buy a drink at a Legion hall, or wander around town wearing a funny hat and have your chest covered in old medals before you can get something with a name like that?

Apparently not.

I had spent five nights in Washington, DC as part of a book tour. The Senate and Congress were in session, an organization of police chiefs was in town, and the largest book industry trade show was in progress. As a result there was no room at the inn.

At least not in the ones I might normally prefer to stay in.

I managed to secure a room in an older hotel a few blocks from the convention center. The room seemed to be clean, although I didn't check every nook and cranny. It had a fairly new bed, a good TV, and an internet connection, which are the top criteria that I normally put on my list when looking for accommodation.

I guess I'm going to have to amend that list.

I now know that I should have checked a few of the nooks and crannies in the air conditioner before turning it on. It was a noisy old window mounted unit that had been installed sometime during the Johnson Administration. I think that might have been Andrew Johnson's administration, not Lyndon's.

As I slept, mold spores too tiny to be seen by the naked eye flew from the cold, dark recesses of the air conditioner and made their way into the warm, dark recesses of my lungs. By the third night, I could no longer sleep. Every time I dozed off, I would awaken within five or ten minutes in a coughing fit.

I assumed that it was just my typical springtime allergies acting up. I normally sneeze and cough my way through the latter half of May, all of June, and the first part of July. I can single-handedly put the manufacturers of antihistamines, facial tissues, and throat lozenges into a profitable financial position in time for their second quarter earnings reports.

By the time I boarded the flight home, I felt like I was breathing by the teaspoonful. It was impossible to take a deep breath without bursting into a lengthy coughing fit. For that matter it was next to impossible to take a normal, or even a shallow breath without the same result.

I was not the most popular passenger on the plane.

When I got home, my doctor prescribed an array of drugs, although none of the fun ones that normally leave me still feeling sick, but not really caring anymore. He also gave me a prescription for one of those inhaler things that sick kids are forever losing at the worst possible moment in made-for-TV movies.

In order to avoid disrupting my wife's sleep, I spent the nights on the living room sofa. It's only fair, because when she is sick, I spend the nights on the living room sofa. Even through sickness, I manage to maintain my role as a freaking saint around here.

At least in my mind...

Pneumonia is not fun. While it may not be fun, there are always a few hidden benefits to everything. For example, pneumonia appears to be great exercise.

After a prolonged coughing fit, all the muscles in my abdomen and chest – the ones I normally shelter under a protective layer of flab – felt like they'd been through two weeks of Marine Corps boot camp.

It even worked on some of the muscle groups that are often ignored by normal exercise regimens. Few people think about the muscles that hold their eyeballs in place. After coughing continuously for five or ten minutes, you'll be glad those muscles are there and doing their jobs. Each coughing fit strengthens them. I was almost convinced that, by the time I'd recover (if I recovered) I'd be able to bench press my body weight just by batting my eyelids.

I was supposed to get lots of rest and drink plenty of fluids. Fun fluids like beer, wine and whiskey weren't on the list. I thought about drinking a bottle of that fluid they gave me before I had a colonoscopy.

It's not that it would do anything ease the pneumonia, but I am sure that within minutes I'd have been afraid to cough.

I'm Stuck Thinking About The "C" Word

We all know what is coming when Labor Day is just a few days away, don't we?

I'm sure there are those of you who think of Labor Day as the harbinger of fall, a return to normalcy, back to school, cooler days, and even cooler nights. Any one of those is a good answer, but, unfortunately, it is not what those fine folks who run retail establishments have in mind.

They know it's time to start getting you geared up for Christmas.

Before you send torch-bearers and crowds with pitchforks stampeding toward my door, I want to make it clear that it isn't me that is bringing up the "C" word so soon. I was in that giant warehouse outlet that uses my surname on all its in-house products the other day, and there on display, in plain view, were Kirkland brand Christmas cards and gift wrap.

I think we must have missed Halloween, or at least we've missed the opportunity to buy Halloween decorations. Mind you, I don't even like the thought of hanging Christmas lights around the roofline, so I am not about to start doing the same thing for Halloween.

In other years I have found it a bit perturbing to see Christmas products on display this early. I know that the first Ho-Ho-Ho will probably be heard within a few weeks, and that also set me off in the past. This year, I almost feel ready for it.

While I don't have any particular desire to set out into the pre-Christmas shopping mall insanity any time soon, and I don't want to hear Nana Mouskouri singing Ave Maria at the best of times, I have spent much of this year with the holiday season near the front of my subconscious. I'm not channeling my inner Santa Claus, even though I have long hair, a white beard, and that whole bowl-full-of-jelly thing working for me when I laugh. I haven't joined a religious cult that spends its time in contemplation of the religious significance of the holiday season.

Still, Christmas has been on my mind. That's what happens when you write a book that is a fictionalized account of some of the things that went on around my home in the late 1950's and early 1960's at Christmastime. As a result, I have spent some of the hottest days of the summer thinking about tobogganing, snowball fights, and the kind of Christmas disasters that could only befall the family that put the "f-u-n" in "dysfunctional." When I look back on the holiday seasons of my childhood, it is those disasters that stand out as the strongest memories. They were the type of disasters or calamities that can best be described as something "we will all laugh about *someday.*"

Around our house we were always taught to see the funnier side of any event, which was one of the major factors that led to my mother's point system for making a sibling pass a liquid or a solid through their sinus cavity at the dinner table. Christmas mealtimes were always prime point generators. Since there was always food of some sort laid out on plates and in bowls around the house at that time of year, the points came throughout the day, as well. I can attest to the fact that mixed salted nuts in the sinuses are something you don't want to experience twice.

In the book, called *The Plight Before Christmas*, I gathered a lot of those disasters and other stories from those days, added some fictionalizing exaggeration, and brought them together into one calamity filled holiday season for a fictional family.

I've heard that thinking about cool things is supposed to help you deal with the heat of an August afternoon. I've spent part of today writing about a 10-year-old kid, trying to clear the driveway before his father gets home from work. He's struggling to keep ahead of the blizzard and the driveway plugging snow plow, and failing miserably. The kid in the story is freezing.

The guy at the keyboard with the "C" word on his mind is still feeling the August heat.

House Parties Are Dangerous When You Are Me

The holiday season is a time for parties, chocolate, and an excuse to imbibe in whatever form of refreshment you choose. Again, and again, and again...

Diane and I went to a house party over the holidays, and when it came time to leave, I was handed my coat, or something that looked a little bit like my coat. It became all too apparent that I had either eaten far too much at the party, or someone of lesser girth had left wearing my coat.

I have often pointed out that I am big for my age; therefore my clothes must be purchased in stores with names like Mr. Humongous, or at the very least from racks hidden near the back of stores for "larger sizes." No one else in attendance at the party came anywhere close to my height or width, so it seemed strange that someone would mistake my coat for theirs.

"No. That has to be your coat," said our host.

Even my wife cast doubts on my ability to tell that I had just put on a coat that belonged on a smaller body, and said, "Are you sure it's not your coat?"

I'm rarely sure of anything, so I did a quick comparison. I arrived wearing a blue coat, and I was trying to fit my body into a much smaller black one. My coat was about a foot longer than the one I was handed, and the imposter coat did not have a hood. In the pocket of the new coat there was a pair of gloves that might have fit on one of my fingers. So yes, I was pretty certain that it was not my coat.

I had a momentary flash of panic when I thought about my car keys, but thankfully I had deposited them into my pants pocket.

I stepped out into the cool night air. No, let me correct that. I stepped out into the freaking cold night air. I hurried to the car, and started the drive home. Wouldn't you just know it. Diane chose that moment to experience one of her "Jeez, it's hot in here moments." She kept turning down the car heat and opening her window. By the time I got home I swear I had icicles on my nipples.

Losing one's coat at a party may be hazardous to your health and wellbeing, but it is nothing when compared with the potential dangers posed by other guests. We were getting ready to leave another party, when an event occurred that left me asking why these things seem to happen to me, but no one else.

As a paraplegic who is trying to stay out of his wheelchair and maneuver through life on crutches clipped to my arms, there are some things that a bit more difficult. One of them is getting up out of a low easy chair in someone's living room.

Diane was standing beside me holding my crutches, while I tried to boost myself out of a chair. It would be a heck of a lot easier if my hosts would be considerate and install a block and tackle above whatever chair I would be using at their parties. There is a point in this process when I will either be upright enough to grip my crutches, or fall backwards into the chair. It's the point when my brother will make a farting noise to make me laugh just so he can watch me collapse back into a chair or car seat. On this occasion, a woman decided to push between Diane and me to hurriedly return to her chair, just as I reached the point of no return.

Her butt, which was straining a pair of black slacks, passed in front of my face about an inch from my nose. It made a good screen for the vision of my life passing before my eyes. I felt like some wayward comet being sucked into a gigantic black hole. I pictured myself being hip-checked into the piano in the corner. I can only be thankful that there were no noises like the ones my brother makes erupting from between her cheeks.

Diane tried to stifle a laugh, as I teetered between maintaining some small degree of poise and collapsing back into the chair. With a look and a few words that I keep in reserve for this sort of situation, I let her know that she had better not start laughing, or I was done for. I said them quietly, through gritted teeth and that just made matters worse.

I grabbed my crutches from her and thrust my arms into the clips, barely managing to stay on my feet. When I had regained some degree of composure, I noticed a couple of the other guests were holding their hands over their mouths, either in shock at what they had just witnessed or, more likely, like Diane, trying to stifle the laughter.

When we reached the car, Diane found she could no longer hold back the laughter any longer. She laughed for the first five miles. When I asked, "Why is always me? Why don't things like this happen to other people?" she broke down even further and told me that I had better find a service station or there was going to be a lot of upholstery shampoo required for her seat.

I knew I really wasn't going to find any sympathy, but I continued to complain about the situation. "I thought for a moment that I had gone blind. All I could see was black."

All I can say now is that I really hope I never experience anything quite like that again, by cracky!

WTF Do They Do There For Excitement?

I have run into some pretty strange town names in my travels. Dildo, Newfoundland in Canada and Toad Suck, Arkansas in the US have to be near the top of any list.

The hands down winner is a little village in Austria, north of Salzburg. I have never personally visited the place, but I was alerted to its existence a few weeks ago. I have no idea what the name translates into in English, but there is little doubt that its name, as it appears on the map, will raise more than a few eyebrows.

I can't imagine what it must be like to be a resident of this village traveling abroad and having to tell some customs officer that you're from Fucking, Austria.

I checked the internet for information about Fucking. You can imagine what I found. (Truth be told, some of what I found was beyond imagination, but that's another story. I'll just say some of those people in the pictures were incredibly limber.) I decided I had better add 'Austria' to my search request. Sure enough, that led me to several sites about the oddly named little town.

From what I learned, much of the town's budget is spent replacing the Fucking town name signs. They are now putting the Fucking signs in cement and welding them to the poles to deter the Fucking sign thieves. In the news item I read, Siegfried Hauppl, the Fucking mayor, is pleading with people to stop stealing the Fucking sign, but he's not having much luck.

"Fucking has existed for 800 years, probably when a Mr. Fuck or the Fuck family moved into the area," he said. "We all know what it means now, but for us, Fucking is Fucking we don't give it a second thought."

I doubt if he is the only Fucking politician with an opinion about it.

In 2004, the 93 Fuckers living in Fucking held an election to decide whether or not to change the name of their town. In the end, they decided that you can't change centuries of Fucking history, and the Fuckers kept the Fucking name.

Perhaps it might help if the sign was reworded. I saw several pictures of the Fucking sign. It says, "Fucking. Bitte – nicht so schnell." In English that's "Fucking. Please - not so fast." Rumor has it that a lot of the thieves are women planning to put it in their bedrooms, but I don't understand why that would be.

I checked the travel site that I use to arrange my air flights and hotels. I couldn't find a Fucking airport or a Fucking hotel. There wasn't even a Fucking car rental agency. I'm sure if the Fuckers could just convince someone to open a Fucking Holiday Inn or even a Fucking Motel Six, it would add a great deal to the Fucking economy.

There doesn't seem to be a Fucking chamber of commerce. I couldn't get any information about the businesses that have chosen to locate there. I'm pretty sure that, as with just about anywhere you might go, there are Fucking bankers. You can be sure that there is at least one Fucking lawyer around there someplace. I seem to recall my friend Roy saying something about his wife's divorce lawyer being one.

Travelers might not steal the Fucking sign so often if some Fucking businessperson opened a Fucking souvenir shop. I think there would be a brisk market for Fucking postcards, Fucking t-shirts, and even those Fucking snow globes. My wife collects souvenir teaspoons. I'm sure she'd like to add one of their Fucking spoons to her collection.

There are a lot of things that the Fucking powers-that-be could do to encourage more Fucking tourism. Austria is noted for its winter sports. Perhaps they could open a Fucking ski hill for tourists to whiz down. There might be a few people who would enjoy the more relaxed pace of a Fucking curling club. I, for one, would happily cheer on a Fucking hockey team. It's been over forty years since my Toronto Maple Leafs won the Stanley Cup. Perhaps they could move there and I would be more accurate when I call them the Fucking Leafs.

I don't know if I will be coming into Fucking anytime soon, but I can always dream, can't I?

This Little Light Of Mine

Camping.

Just the word can send a shudder up my spine. It's a memory induced automatic reaction. Camping and shivering seem to go hand in hand, even during the hottest days of the summer, cold nights in a sleeping bag can prove that involuntary shivering is, in fact, an aerobic exercise.

Needless to say I am neither enamored with nor very good at camping. It just seems like a very expensive way to prove that you can survive homelessness. Well, maybe you can, but I'm not so sure about my survival potential.

I have on occasion, been forced to throw caution to the wind and give camping a try. A number of years ago, my son was playing hockey in a town 250 miles from home. Hockey and camping would normally be in separate seasons, however Brad played hockey twelve months of the year. On this particular occasion he was on the ice in mid-July.

Something in my brain may have malfunctioned. I made the mistake of thinking that it might be OK to give camping another try in order to watch him play. To this day I cannot drive along that stretch of highway without having a flashback to my memorable and enlightening camping escapades.

When I had my campsite all set up, with a gas stove warming a pot of beans, I sat back and admired my abilities to be prepared, even though I had never been a Boy Scout. Aside from the stove, I had my air mattress inflated, my sleeping bag laid out on top of it, and a somewhat comfortable folding chair facing the lake a few feet away from the tent. A flock of ducks swam back and forth along the shoreline, hoping that I might share something with them. To complete the pastoral scene of man bonding with nature, the sun started to set behind a mountain.

That's when I realized that I had forgotten something. I had a small flashlight for making the trip to the outhouse a few campsites away, but I had no source of light for the campsite after dark.

I turned off the pot of beans, and jumped into the car for a short drive into town where I had seen a store that specialized in car repairs, hand tools and camping equipment. It was obviously not the sort of place I normally frequented, but I was pretty sure I could find a lantern of some description.

They had kerosene lanterns that looked like a fast route to third degree burns and skin graft surgery. They had an array of flashlights, that didn't seem to be much better than the one I had.

And then I found it.

On display at the end of an aisle was a great looking lamp. I had an electrical hook-up at the campsite, so it would be a simple matter of running an extension cord from it to this wondrous lamp. I knew it was perfect for my needs, mainly because on the side of the box it said "perfect for home workshops, car repair, and camping."

By the time I got back from my shopping trip, dusk had fallen. I sat in my chair and unpacked the lamp from its box. I managed to find the electrical outlet, and surprisingly without shocking myself into the middle of the next week, I got the extension cord plugged in on just my third try. I connected the lamp to the other end of the cord, and flicked its switch.

What happened next is a bit of a blur.

The lamp lit up my campsite, and three neighboring states.

Acrid smoke started to rise from it, which I quickly determined was from the flesh on my fingers burning off.

Campers throughout the park stopped singing around their campfires. Several of them told me in no uncertain terms what I should do with the lamp. I would have turned it off, but the light was so bright I couldn't look at the thing and I had forgotten where to find the switch.

Their comments were rather rude. You would think they might have shown some appreciation for the fact that every mosquito, moth, and gnat was making a beeline for my campsite, and away from theirs.

The ducks woke from their evening slumber and started quacking at me. I think I know what they were saying. One of them took off from the lakeshore and crashed into a tree.

A group of evangelical Christians a couple of campsites away started shouting something about the rapture arriving ahead of schedule. When they saw my long-haired, bearded silhouette rise up in the light three of them fainted on the spot.

I think I may have thrown off the solar instrumentation on the International Space Station.

I stumbled around the campsite trying to find the extension cord, but all I could see was the outline of the lamp that had been burned into my retinas. I tripped over a guy wire causing both me and the tent to collapse in a heap. I used a few special words that were very similar to the ones I was hearing from people on the other side of the two-mile wide lake in their description of the light.

As I crawled on the ground I found the extension cord. Ignoring all of the teachings of my father about how to properly pull a cord from a socket, I jerked on it until it freed itself from the outlet, thrusting the entire area back into sweet darkness.

I lay on the ground for several minutes. I think I was staring at the sky, but I was so disoriented I could have been facing the ground for all I knew. The campground had become very quiet. There was just a slight sizzling noise coming from a few feet away, which I assumed to be the lamp boiling the last remnants of dew off the blades of grass. For all I cared at that point, it could have been one of the area's rattle snakes slithering blindly through the grass.

Just before the campground owner stopped by to suggest that I find other accommodations in the morning, I heard the Christians talking to him. They were using words like 'satanic' and 'Antichrist.'. I think the ducks were having the same thoughts.

When I was packing up in the morning, amid the glares of several other campers, I thought about picking up the lamp, but I swear it growled at me.

Does Medicare Pay Amateur Physicians?

I'm always amazed at how many amateur doctors there are out there. I'm not talking about the people who sit in the front row of strip clubs giving complimentary breast and gynecological examinations. I'm referring to the people who are convinced, despite any formal medical training, that they know what's wrong with you, what you can and can't do, and what you should do about every conceivable -- and sometimes inconceivable -- ailment, injury, or symptom.

While I realize that there may be certain shortages in the medical field, I don't think turning to cocktail-circuit amateurs is the best way to avoid overcrowded doctors' offices and hospitals.

It has now been over twenty years since the accident that left me with reduced mobility, limitations on my lifestyle, and chronic pain.

There has also been a level of pain that really had nothing to do with the accident. That's the chronic pain in the butt from people who think they know what is best for me. They don't seem to care if their diagnoses have any basis in fact. They just like to share their medical assumptions with the world.

I have no trouble accepting the fact that doctors can be mistaken. Since the accident, I've received both good and bad medical care. Some of the doctors I've run across have been perfect examples of the adage that half of all doctors were in the bottom 50% of their graduating classes. I can still hear the hospital emergency department doctor, who I don't think had reached puberty at the time, telling me that there was no bone damage done in the accident that left me disabled. He failed to see the broken ribs, and more importantly failed to have x-rays taken of my entire spine, thereby missing the spinal injury.

That experience left me wondering if I could have something engraved on a Medic Alert bracelet that says, even if I'm found at death's door, not to take me back to that particular hospital.

I feel fortunate to have my current family doctor. I feel unfortunate to have a hoard of prying amateur medical hobbyists, who think they can out-diagnose everyone from the local pharmacist to the Mayo Clinic. These amateurs seem to specialize in all branches of medical science. They are willing to diagnose everything from a head cold to the latest condition they read about on the Internet.

I'm always dreading the day when I might encounter an amateur proctologist.

Amateur dieticians are equally bad. I've been told I should eat grapefruit, drink wine, avoid grapefruit, abstain from any alcohol, eat lots of carbohydrates, don't eat any carbohydrates, and every other contrary opinion about food you could think of. Naturally, there are lots of people who tell me that I shouldn't eat red meat. I don't eat a lot of red meat. After it's cooked it is usually more of gray-brown color. Personally I think people should avoid eating meat that is green, and just to be on the safe side, stay away from other green foods like broccoli and Brussels sprouts.

Underlying all of this gratuitous, unwanted advice, these amateur physicians are really indicating that I am probably too stupid to seek out the appropriate medical treatments. I will readily admit to being stupid about a lot of things. My immediate family would probably be willing to give you a detailed list of my intellectual insufficiencies if you have a couple of days to listen to them.

Despite these failings, I know more about my physical wellbeing than they do. My medical advisors also know more about my physical wellbeing than they do. Together, we don't need help from people whose only medical knowledge comes from the pages of grocery store tabloids, TV soap operas, and, of course, the ever popular, "I have a friend, who has a friend, who has the same problem you do..."

There are even amateur faith healers. I was told by one woman that I needed to search deep within my soul to determine what evil I had committed to make God punish me with the injury. If I made amends for that I would be instantly cured. Another woman told me that I needed to learn how to pray better, so that I could ask God to take away the injury.

I could try a prayer to take away that particular pain, something along the lines of "Dear God: Please save me from your idiotic followers."

If I put my mind to it I could probably come up with a few diagnosis of my own about the people who feel the need to meddle in other people's health-related business. I'm sure I could be at least as accurate about their medical conditions as they are about mine, but that would just make me an amateur psychiatrist.

On the other hand, perhaps I should listen to them, or better yet, I could use same sources of medical knowledge that they do, and come up with a self-diagnosis. Who needs several years of medical school when you've got the internet to turn to?

Let's see, I don't have much patience for people, especially those that want to tell me what's wrong with me. I have difficulty standing up from a chair. I sometimes feel sick to my stomach. I regularly have cravings for chocolate, peanut butter, and Fig Newtons®. Sometimes I crave Fig Newtons® covered with chocolate and peanut butter. My waistline is quite a bit larger than it used to be…

…Oh, Good Lord. I must be pregnant.

A Family Can Turn You Green

To quote one of the greatest philosophers of the 20th Century, Kermit The Frog, "It's not easy being green."

Family life is enough to turn the most environmentally concerned individual into a living, breathing ecological disaster. When I was younger I was very involved in the anti-pollution movement and active in wildlife preservation. Having a family made it far more difficult to keep hiking on the straight and narrow environmental trail.

I became environ-mentally challenged.

When our sons were babies, we didn't follow the trend toward disposable diapers. Oh no, not us. We stayed true to the environment and used cloth diapers. Looking back, I'm not entirely sure how helpful we were being. Every second day, we had to lug the diaper pail to the laundry room.

"It's diaper day," became some of the most feared words I could hear coming from my wife's mouth. While 'we' used cloth diapers, and 'we' washed them ourselves rather than sending them to a diaper service, it was most definitely 'I' who did the lugging of the pail and exposing himself to toxic fumes when lifting the pail's lid. I remain convinced that opening that lid was largely responsible for the hole in the ozone layer, acid rain, global warming, and a peculiar little facial tick I still have whenever anyone mentions the word 'diaper.'

It was enough to make me environ-mentally ill.

I started thinking about the benefits of disposable, non-biodegradable, landfill clogging disposable diapers. I left grocery store coupons for them in conspicuous places. My wife never took the hint, but eventually, after close to five years, and over 900 times hearing my wife utter those three little words – "It's diaper day," our sons were toilet trained.

It would be nice to think that our home could reduce its environmental impact after that, but small boys tend to undergo a metamorphosis. They become teenage boys. I'm convinced that the average fifteen-year-old boy can produce as much global warming methane gas as an entire herd of Brazilian beef cattle.

My generation blamed the previous one for the pollution and the rest of the world's ills. My sons blame us for the same thing. I recall getting a lengthy lecture from one of the boys about all of the ills that his generation would have to clean up, because of the impact baby boomers were having on the environment. At the time, I was driving with my head stuck out the side window trying to breathe, because he was sitting in his sweaty, post-game hockey gear, single-handedly raising the entire province's smog alert level.

Forget the toxic footprint. He left a toxic buttprint in my passenger seat.

One of our sons once begged us for a hamster to keep in his room. Even though we had already experienced his lack of willingness to deal with a polluted cat litter pan, we eventually relented. We bought a cage, wood shavings, and a small furry beast. The smell in his room was absolutely unbelievable, but eventually the hamster got used to it and stopped trying to escape.

A teenage boy's room is something that should only be entered if you are wearing a hazmat suit. One never knows just what type of chemical soup is festering in there. Dirty laundry shoved in corners of the closet, dishes hidden under the bed with mold growing entirely new civilizations, and backpacks holding several uneaten sandwiches from the previous school year all combine to create something far worse than anything you might find in a toxic waste dump.

On one hand, Kermit the Frog was right. When you are dealing with the demands of raising sons, and living in a family, it's not very easy to be green. On the other hand, whenever I think back on all those diaper pails, the sweaty hockey equipment, and the state of teenage boys' bedrooms, it's pretty easy to turn a little green.

It's Just A Dream... I Hope

I'm really not too sure about this dream interpretation thing. I just read an article about it, and I have to admit, it left me feeling more than a little confused.

Apparently if you dream about eating prunes, you might be expecting to change residences soon. OK, hands up. Who here has ever dreamt about eating prunes? If I eat prunes, it might make me want to change rooms in a hurry, but unless I don't make it from the living room to that other room, I don't think it would make me want to change residences.

"Sorry about the stain the size and shape of Rhode Island on the carpet, dear. Let's just call the real estate agent."

The article also stated that if you dream about polar bears, good fortune is headed your way. I've watched those documentaries on the National Geographic channel. I've seen what a polar bear can do to a seal with one swipe of its paw. If I dream about a polar bear the good fortune will be that I wake up before it catches me.

If I woke up screaming, "AAAAAAARRRRRRGGGHHHH! It's going to eat me!" because a polar bear is chasing me through dream land, the good fortune would be not getting killed in real life. Diane hates it when I wake her up screaming," AAAAAAARRRRRRGGGHHHH! It's going to eat me!" At least now I might have some good news to calm her down.

"Sorry dear. It was a polar bear in my dream. As soon as you get down from clinging to the ceiling fan, let's go buy a lottery ticket. I think good fortune is headed my way."

If you dream that you can't find your house, it is supposed to mean that you are uncertain about your life path. Yeah, right. I know people who can't find their house from the end of their block without referring to a GPS device. The only thing they are uncertain about is how much they had to drink before heading home. Forget uncertainty walking along their life path. They're uncertain walking along the sidewalk.

Supposedly, you can expect success in your current undertakings if you dream about a llama. Again, hands up if you dream ever dream about llamas. (OK, a few of you Scots might dream about your sheep, but that doesn't count, you perverted Highland ewe-bangers.)

On the other hand, not dreaming about llamas provides a great excuse for any failure you might have.

"Well, dear, I failed at my attempt to develop a personal nuclear power plant out in the garage, but I haven't been dreaming about llamas so it's not really my fault that we no longer have a garage... a driveway... neighbors... the cat... "

Dreaming about blackbirds means that your life will be dull and boring. Of course it does. You're dreaming about blackbirds, for crying out loud. How much duller can things get?

"I dreamt about blackbirds last night, and now I have an insatiable urge to watch my DVD collection of seasons one through twenty-eight of The Price Is Right."

The article said you should write down what you dream about as soon as you wake up. That way, when you are fully awake, you can either determine what it really means, or you can think about it again before going to sleep the next night to experience or remember more of the dream.

I tried that and now I'm afraid to go to sleep again. When I looked at the notepad beside my bed the other morning I found that I had written something quite disturbing.

I don't think I want to know what "Harry Truman is wearing a negligee" means.

All My Actions Can Have An Unequal And Unpredictable Reaction

We really are creatures of habit. We expect that every action will have an equal and predictable reaction. If we put money in a vending machine, we expect to get our selection based on the button we push. If we don't want buttons pushed, we don't expect inanimate objects to push them for us.

Unless you are me.

For some reason equal and predictable reactions elude me.

Diane and I were in an airport a few months ago, and I decided to make use of the restroom before boarding the airplane and subjecting myself to trying to fit an extra-large body into a petite size lavatory. As I sat, I noticed the vending machine on the wall.

One of the selections was for a temporary tattoo featuring Disney's Tigger from Winnie The Pooh. Diane has always been a big fan of Tigger.

I've told you before about our oldest son's nursery. It was decorated with a Winnie the Pooh motif. The wallpaper joints were in Pooh's leg and Tigger's tail. They matched up well at the top of the wall, but by the bottom it looked like Pooh had a compound fracture and Tigger had caught his tail in a car door.

I thought Diane would get a kick out of a Tigger temporary tattoo, although I wasn't quite sure where she would put it. I fed some coins into the machine and pushed the button under the grinning face of Tigger.

I didn't get a Tigger tattoo. I got a tampon.

At least I finally figured out what it was. After opening the little package expecting to see a Tigger tattoo, I thought I had mistakenly gotten a cheap cardboard yo-yo. No matter how hard I tried, I couldn't get it to go up and down on the sting. It eventually shed its cardboard tubing and I discovered what was inside.

In the words of husbands everywhere who have found themselves holding one of those things, "Ewwwwww! Gross!"

Someone had obviously rearranged the signs indicating what each portion of the machine dispensed.

I suppose my luck could have been worse. I could have been an unsuspecting woman feeding her last bit of change into the machine in an emergency situation. I can image her reaction if she got a Tigger tattoo instead of a tampon. That would definitely be a deal with no strings attached.

Sometimes I get unexpected and unpredictable reactions when other buttons get pushed.

As I mentioned, airplane lavatories and I are not made for each other. I think that if the fun folks at Boeing or McDonnell Douglas put their minds to it, they could actually make those little rooms smaller. Aside from my height and width making it difficult to maneuver, add in the fact that I walk with crutches.

I really try to avoid using airplane lavatories, but on a five-hour flight, my two-hour bladder objects strenuously to the idea of waiting until I get back into an airport.

On a recent flight, I made my way into a lavatory, and propped my crutches against the wall when I was uncomfortably seated. It's been my longstanding belief that pilots seek out turbulence when they are aware that I have entered a lavatory, and this occasion would be no different.

The plane shook and bounced, and one of my crutches fell forward. Before I could catch it, the hand grip of the crutch hit the flush button on the wall. The next few minutes are forever etched into my mind.

Cold, blue disinfectant shot out beneath me like a malfunctioning bidet. I had heard stories of people getting wedged onto airplane toilet seats in situations like that, and I could feel the suction building beneath me as the cold spray fired up at me. I was madly trying to keep my dripping hind quarters from getting stuck to the seat. I didn't notice that my crutch was still pressing the flush button until the whole demonic process started over again.

I felt so disinfected.

Icy blue liquid was running down my leg and I was trying to stop its flow with handfuls of paper towels before it could reach my tan pants on the floor. I pictured myself looking like a Smurf thanks to the blue dye in the disinfectant.

When I bent forward I smashed the top of my head into the door. Thankfully it didn't fly open or several rows of passengers would have been distracted away from the inflight movie by an inflight me.

At least they wouldn't have seen a strategically positioned temporary Tigger tattoo.

Hopefully When He Becomes A Doctor He'll Have A Roof Over His Head.

Parents love to brag about the accomplishments of their children. Dinner parties seem to be prime locales for passing along the accolades about the people they passed their genes to many years earlier.

I joined in the brag fest a while back by pointing out that my youngest son is currently in England studying to be a doctor. There were approving nods around the room, filling me with pride for having produced such brilliance from my X and Y chromosomes. Diane may have had something to do with it, too.

Someone asked if he was specializing or if he would be a general practitioner.

"Oh, he's very specialized," I replied, amid more approving glances, and a few that seemed to be tinted with a hint of jealousy.

"Cancer? Neurology? Gynecology?" they asked.

"The armorers of England in the twelfth and thirteenth centuries," I said.

Those approving glances turned to something that might have indicated that the people suddenly realized I was from a different planet.

Brad is doing a doctorate in Medieval Studies at the University of York in the United Kingdom, although it wasn't all that united during the period he is studying.

If someone ever asks, "Is there a doctor in the house?" Brad will be able to say that he is indeed a doctor, but he could only help by telling them what type of armor might have helped prevent the gaping wound in the patient.

Brad was the first member of our family to earn a Master's Degree. His dissertation was about the man who was the mayor of London in 1380. The political intrigue that was involved in his rise to power would have made Richard Nixon look like a rank amateur. Brad decided to stay on in York to do his doctorate, and teach undergraduate history students.

A few weeks ago, Brad was the first member of the family to have another, less impressive experience. In fact I cannot think of another person I have ever heard of who has had this particular experience.

Someone stole his roof.

The whole roof.

And nothing but the roof.

Brad and Deb live in a flat in a building that is about 350 years old. It has, or rather had, a roof made from lead panels. Someone managed to get up on their roof and steal all of the lead panels. It's similar to what Cromwell did to the abbeys scattered around that part of England, when he needed lead for his muskets.

Questions sprang to my mind. Who would steal a roof? Why would someone steal a roof? How could someone steal a roof without being noticed? Where is Santa Claus going to land at Brad's house?

Apparently there is good money to be made these days from stealing metal. Someone near our house stole over a mile of telephone cable right off the poles in order to get the copper out of it. They sell it to scrap metal dealers, who in turn sell it to people who use the metal. I bet there is a roofer in England right now with some lead panels that he picked up at Hot Lead R Us that will fit Brad's roof perfectly.

Brad inherited my interest in literature and history. That will serve him well in his studies. He also inherited my handyman skills. That will do diddly-squat to solve his missing roof problem. I did, however, give him my favorite power tool for Christmas this year. He can use the eight-inch reciprocating telephone receiver to call his landlord and discuss his missing roof.

I Hate Those Fish-Lip Kisses

A few years ago, Diane and I took up snorkeling and underwater photography as something to get us away from our offices. Since the Pacific Ocean is right on our doorstep, we obviously decided to do it in the Caribbean. It's not that I have anything against the Pacific, it's just that the water temperature around here averages something like 10 degrees Celsius (50 degrees Fahrenheit for those of you who are metrically challenged.)

There is also that problem with disembodied feet washing up on our shoreline all too frequently. I prefer to swim without skeletal remains, thank you very much. No one is sure why we are having an influx of feet in running shoes hitting the sand like messages in the bottle. I, of course, have a theory.

Several years ago, a doctor in the United States was disciplined because he had used a patient's amputated foot as bait in a crab trap. Crabbing is a popular pastime in these waters and we have a lot of doctors around here. Put two and two together.

We got our first taste of the joys of snorkeling and taking pictures of the undersea world a few years ago in Grand Cayman. One of our stops was a sandbar teeming with southern sting rays. The minute we got into the water, we were surrounded by rays. Diane was having images of the late Steve Irwin flash before her eyes. (Irwin was killed by a stingray the year before.)

Our guide handed me a dead squid and told me to hold it underwater like an ice cream cone, and be careful not to let the stingray grab my thumb. I went underwater holding the squid away from my body. A huge ray swam up and sucked it right out of my hand. Naturally, it also sucked my thumb into its mouth.

I rode for a good twenty-five feet like a deep sea hitchhiker, pulled along by the ray. Eventually he spit out my thumb and I was able to resurface.

I stood on a sand bar catching my breath, which involved coughing out a gallon or so of sea water. The same ray circled back to see if I had anything else to eat. He swam right into my arms.

Our guide said, "Don't worry, Mon. Kiss him. You'll get seven years of good luck."

Right. I'm going to kiss a… That's when the rest of our "friends" on the boat started chanting "Kiss it! Kiss it! Kiss it!" I was about to tell them what I thought of the idea and all of them at that particular moment when one of them threw in a double dog dare. I was immediately doomed to partake in a feat of man/fish osculation, because one cannot avoid the double dog dare.

I started to pucker up, when the guide said, "and if you slip him a bit of tongue, you'll get 100 years of good luck."

I decided that I could return to Grand Cayman in seven years and recharge my luck.

Thankfully The Sharks Weren't In The Mood For Pâté de Gord Gras

Whether we admit it or not, we all have some form of a bucket list; things we would like to do before we kick our buckets. One of the items high on my list was to swim with sharks.

Our first encounter with a shark came in a secluded inlet on the north side of the island of St. John in the U.S. Virgin Islands. We had chartered a sailboat to take us out to a few snorkeling sites away from the areas normally visited by tourists.

As Diane was returning to the boat, a small shark swam beneath her. She had already removed her mask and was getting ready to get out of the water, so I knew she was unaware of her visitor. I managed to get a photograph showing just her legs, the ladder on the boat, and the shark. I didn't show it to her until we were back on dry land.

I stayed in the water after Diane got back onto the boat, trying to get a few more pictures of the shark, which had been joined by a few buddies. Because she was unaware of just what I was swimming with, Diane decided to feed the seagulls who were circling the boat, no doubt waiting for the sharks to leave some meat behind. I was hoping it wouldn't be my meat, but thankfully they decided that I was probably not up to their normal quality standards.

The sharks busied themselves with grabbing at the bits of snack mix Diane was throwing overboard. When I surfaced, planning to tell her that I would prefer she not start a feeding frenzy in my immediate vicinity, I broke the surface, just as a seagull landed to grab a pretzel that was now resting on the top of my head. The collision was undoubtedly quite spectacular.

This was not the first time I had collided with something when surfacing. Many years earlier, at our summer home north of Toronto, Diane and my father had thrown a tennis ball for our dog. My head popped up just as the tennis ball plopped down. My first thought was that I had surfaced beneath one of the lakes snapping turtles.

I have now proven without a shadow of a doubt that when I collide with something when surfacing, I can scream like a little girl. Of course that also fills my lungs with water, and I can cough and choke like an old man.

One of the attractions along the coral reef in Belize is an area called Shark/Ray Alley. The area is teeming with fish, and as you might guess from its name, stingrays and sharks. We were already pretty comfortable being in the water with stingrays, having snorkeled with them in Grand Cayman, St. Kitts, and St. Thomas. I was expecting to see sharks about the same size as the little one I saw off St. John.

I certainly wasn't expecting to see one that was almost nine feet long, and I definitely wasn't expecting it to swim alongside me for several minutes. I was fascinated by him. I think he had the idea that I might like to go with him and kill something. He stayed so close to me I could have touched him without extending my arm, but I decided that might not be the wisest move. After all, I didn't want the guide telling me that I should kiss him for luck.

Along with the sharks there was another species of fish. Horse-eye Jack fish get their name from their eyes, which seem about fifteen sizes too big for their bodies. They stay close to the sharks, hoping to get scraps of whatever the sharks are eating. One of them lost patience waiting for a meal, so it swam up and bit me on the back of my hand.

Wouldn't you just know that this would be the time I went into the water without my gloves?

I looked at my hand and saw the outline of the fish's mouth. I calmly and coolly thought, "Oh look... I'm bleeding... in the water... WITH A SHARK THREE FEET AWAY!"

Thankfully, there was not enough blood to get my new found friend excited, and we continued swimming, although I covered the bite with my other hand just to be on the safe side.

As we were returning to the boat, I saw two young hammerhead sharks in the distance. Hammerheads are not as friendly as the sand tiger sharks I had been swimming with, and I decided to get out of the water without pausing for one last look around. They are quite convenient sharks, though. Their heads are like handle bars that you can hold onto while they eat you.

After our encounters with the sand tiger sharks, I thought it might be OK to suggest to Diane that we up the ante on a future trip and head to someplace where we could swim with great whites.

I'm always amazed at just how wide Diane's eyes can open when she gives me her patented deer-in-the-headlights look that clearly conveys the message that she thinks I am off my rocker.

Dogs That Have Owned Me

My canine assistant, Tara hates fireworks and thunderstorms. At the first sound of either one, she will go into the bathroom, jump into the tub, and pull the shower curtain closed with her teeth. She sits in the empty tub panting furiously. It's remarkably similar to what my wife does if she sees a spider.

Our community banned fireworks for personal use a few years ago. It's a fairly strict bylaw, but unfortunately, the bylaw enforcement officer doesn't work at night, when it would seem to be the prime time for firework detonation.

I have never understood why, but for some reason fireworks are set off around here on Halloween. It's a great combination, overly sugared children and explosives. The community also sets off fireworks after the annual community festival, and you can be guaranteed that some yahoo or another will set off a few at midnight on New Year's Eve.

I don't recall any of my other dogs reacting quite that way at the sound of fireworks or thunder, but all of them have had their own quirks that made them unique.

Our first dog was a border collie. Like so many of his breed, he lived to chase whatever you were willing to throw for him, and, if you weren't in a throwing mood, he would decide to herd whatever he could. We would often see our two cats, running through the house with every hair on their bodies standing on end. Right behind them would be the dog herding them from the living room to the bedroom and back again. He even made friends with a raccoon that lived in the small bush on our property, He would run the raccoon into the bush, and a moment later, the raccoon would reciprocate by chasing him back out of the bush.

It was a particularly memorable day, when he decided to try herding a skunk in the predawn darkness. It was made even more memorable when my olfactory-challenged wife didn't realize what he had done, and let him back into the house.

Border collies are noted for their intelligence. One of his favourite toys was a plastic flying disk that he would bring to whomever he thought he could convince to throw it. He would watch the angle of the disk as it left your hand, and run, not after the disk, but to the spot he determined it would end up.

He was five years old by the time our first son arrived, and he saw the miniature human as someone who had usurped his place in the pecking order of our family pack.

Mike had a small rubber toy that he particularly liked, and for some reason it kept disappearing. We never saw the dog with it, so we didn't blame him. We would just go out and buy a replacement. Other toys would disappear from time to time, but none with the regularity of the small rubber blue elephant. When we moved, we lifted the box spring of our bed and heard an odd rattling noise. The material on the bottom had a small tear. Inside the box spring we found sever blue rubber elephants, toy cars, and a teddy bear that the dog had hidden there. He didn't want the toys for himself, but he sure didn't want Mike to have them either.

We added a second dog to the household a year after the border collie arrived. He was a beautiful dog, half Newfoundland and have husky. Unfortunately, he as all stupid.

We had a maple tree that grew out of the side of a small hill at an odd angle. One day I found the dog halfway up the tree. He had run up the trunk as if it was a ramp, probably chasing one of the cats. "Dogs don't climb trees," I said to him.

With that he looked at me and promptly fell out of the tree.

That dog didn't stay with us for long. He developed a habit of breaking free from his leash and visiting a farm down the road. The Russian farmer had a large flock of chickens, and the dog would come home with one whenever he felt a bit peckish.

One day I answered the door. The Russian farmer was there with a rifle in his hand. "I kill your dog if you don't get rid of him. He's eating my birds."he said, shaking his rifle in front of me. I was about to deny the charges, when the dog rounded the corner of the house with a feather sticking out of his mouth.

It's hard to defend a chicken thief when he is coughing up feathers at your feet. We found him a new home away from chicken farms.

We next adopted a Labrador-Irish Setter cross. He and the border collie played well together. He was a gorgeous dog, black with red highlights, but again, what he had in looks was offset by a severe shortage of working brain cells.

They would run through the corn field behind our house by the hour, chasing rabbits and whatever else they could find back there. When we would call them, the border collie, despite being quite a bit shorter in the leg department, would always be the first one home. I'm sure he hurried just in case it meant that someone had something that needed to be thrown and retrieved. The other dog would come galloping down the hill, and a few feet from the back wall of the house he would realize that he didn't have room to stop. I'm sure he suffered several concussions in his collisions with the wall, and the siding on the house bore several deep dents indicating his target points.

On one rather spectacular occasion he missed the house, but ran into the back of the car. Try explaining a large dent in your car to an insurance adjuster by saying your dog hit the car.

We eventually gave him away to a home without a hill, and hopefully his headaches abated.

My earlier books had several stories detailing the life of our next dog. Nipper was a blond cocker spaniel. She was a loyal and loving dog, but was dumber than a sack full of rusty nails. She had some working brain cells, but only the ones that were used for things like putting one foot in front of the other, or knowing when someone had brought a pizza into the house. I often referred to her as the dumbest dog to ever get lost on a single flight of stairs, because, quite frankly, she could get lost halfway between the ground floor and the main floor of the house, and we would have to come and rescue a whimpering, trembling pile of cocker spaniel.

So Tara may have her idiosyncrasies about fireworks or thunderstorms, but she brings an incredible amount of joy to our lives. She's also the smartest dog we have ever owned, which, with the exception of the border collie, isn't saying much.

In her role as my canine assistant, she can open and close doors, pick up anything I drop, bring beer from the kitchen to my chair in the living room, and, perhaps most noteworthy, rescue anyone who has been left with an empty toilet paper roll by bringing a fresh supply from the hall closet.

Several women have told me that they wish their husbands would learn to do that, including my wife.

CPSIA information can be obtained at www.ICGtesting.com
Printed in the USA
LVOW10s1804100315

429965LV00036B/1265/P